DEADLY UFOS
AND
THE DISAPPEARED

By
Rob Shelsky

Deadly UFOS, Aliens, And The Disappeared

PUBLISHED BY:
GKRS PUBLICATIONS
Copyright © 2015 by Rob Shelsky
Smashwords Edition
Cover Artwork By Illustrator Joshua Higgins

All rights reserved. Without limiting the rights under copyright reserved above, no part of this publication may be reproduced, stored in or introduced into a retrieval system, or transmitted, in any form, or by any means (electronic, mechanical, photocopying, recording, or otherwise) without the prior written permission of both the copyright owners and the above publisher of this book.

This is a work of nonfiction. The authors acknowledge the trademarked status and trademark owners of various products referenced in this work of nonfiction, which have been used without permission. The publication/use of these trademarks is not authorized, associated with, or sponsored by the trademark owners. All quotations and/or related materials are referenced either in the body of this book itself, or referenced at the end.

Citation Notes:

All works cited herein have their sources included. All illustrations/photos are courtesy Wikimedia Commons and/or other Public Domain images. Short portions of Public Domain documents, such as the Bible, etc., as well as short Public Domain quotations by scientists, researchers, and others have been reproduced herein.

* * * * *

DEDICATED
IN MEMORIAM
TO

~ *GEORGE A. KEMPLAND* ~

Author, Friend, And So Very Much More.
1929 — 2013

*Wherever You Are Now, George,
May You Always Be Happy, At Peace, And Enjoy
Yourself.
I Hope I May Get To See you Again...Somewhen.*

CONTENTS

INTRODUCTION—ARE WE VICTIMS?..1
PART 1—THE GREAT UFO CONSPIRACY—AN OVERVIEW 6
CHAPTER 1—THE GREAT UFO CONSPIRACY THEORY 7
CHAPTER 2—EXTENT OF THE COVERUP?....................................17
CHAPTER 3—HOW FAR WOULD OUR GOVERNMENT GO?........33
CHAPTER 4—JUST WHAT ARE UFOS? 47
PART 2—UFOS—THE KILLING FIELDS..58
CHAPTER 5—DAMAGE CAUSED BY UFOS 59
CHAPTER 6—INJURIES 63
CHAPTER 7—UFOS KILLING PEOPLE?..83
CHAPTER 8—MILITARY DEATHS RELATED TO UFOS................106
CHAPTER 9—DEATHS OF INVESTIGATORS &RESEARCHERS.....115
CHAPTER 10—GIGANTIC UFOS? 145
PART 3—THE TRULY BIZARRE...153
CHAPTER 11—DEADLY FORBIDDEN ZONES?...........................154
CHAPTER 12—ABDUCTIONS...162
CHAPTER 13—CROP CIRCLES..170
CHAPTER 14—ANIMAL MUTILATIONS.....................................177
PART 4—MYSTERY OF THE DISAPPEARED! 186
CHAPTER 15—THE DISAPPEARED—INDIVIDUALS 187
CHAPTER 16—DISAPPEARANCE OF GROUPS OF PEOPLE 208
CHAPTER 17—DISAPPEARANCE OF VILLAGES AND MORE 217
CONCLUSION 233
ABOUT THE AUTHOR 254
REFERENCES 256

INTRODUCTION—ARE WE VICTIMS?

Deadly UFOs, Aliens, and the Disappeared. Some people witness UFOs and find the sight of them intriguing, enthralling, or even awe-inspiring. However, given time, they then move on with their lives, as most people tend to do. The memory of the event, although not lost, diminishes in importance over the days and years to come. In other words, "life goes on."

This is not always the case. Sometimes, viewing such objects will result in fundamentally changing the witness's life. Major alterations can occur in the viewpoint of such individuals, and forevermore, so profound is the effect upon them of seeing such things. This is often to the point where many researchers of the phenomenon say that some who witness such events actually have a sort of transcendental or religious reaction. In other words, "they get religion," as one researcher put it. The "religion" isn't of the usual variety, but more often than not, a hybrid version of what the person once believed. So psychological aftereffects, whether these are for the better or not, and that is a matter of individual interpretation, do occur.

Moreover, with most UFO sightings, witnesses of such objects suffer no ill consequences, other than, perhaps in some cases, psychological ones. The exact nature of this psychological damage, the long-term effects on the psyche of individuals is often hard to measure and determine.

However, others do suffer actual physical injuries, sometimes severe in nature. These are, of course, therefore a measurable effect upon the witness. Moreover, still others die, sometimes alone and horribly, but sometimes in groups, as well. Not only is the death of such people of major importance to all of us, but one cannot underestimate the impact of such events on their immediate family and friends. This is usually devastating.

This may seem hard to believe, difficult for the average individual even to countenance as really happening, the idea that UFOs or extraterrestrials may actually cause such terrible things, but the evidence for this is there. It seems incontrovertible in many cases. UFOs, it seems, can and sometimes do injure and kill, and much more often than most people might realize. These strange craft flying in our skies also seem to cause something else, something far more sinister in a way, and that is disappearances.

I'm not just talking about abductions here, those people who experience missing time and claim to have suffered painful and invasive alien examinations, and then return to us. I mean permanent disappearances. Furthermore, it isn't just a case of the odd individual who disappears, but again, groups, as well.

Sometimes, the populations of entire villages have vanished, never to be seen again. People disappear in broad daylight, in front of eyewitnesses. Moreover, this has happened historically, as well as recently. The phenomenon appears to be not only of long duration, but an ongoing one, as well. The evidence for this happening seems considerable.

So, just what does all this mean for humanity? Why has this happened in the past and is still happening to us now? What does this sort of thing portend for us as individuals and as a species? In short, the question must be asked: **WHAT IS HAPPENING TO US?**

In this book, I will discuss all of the above-mentioned subjects, separately and together. I will cite a number of actual case histories for each category, but I will limit these, since I am of the firm belief that "more isn't always better." Either such cases will convince, or they will not, and citing endless cases will not help in this regard.

In addition, I will discuss the circumstances of these instances, whether or not such events have enough evidence to make them convincing examples of the phenomena I am discussing here in this book.

Furthermore, I will attempt to answer some of the above questions. The most important of these questions, being, "What's going on?" We all need to know, not only what is going on, but why it's happening. Lastly, we want to know what it portends for us all, because these cases don't happen just in certain isolated regions, but worldwide, everywhere. Moreover, the number of occurrences of them is on the rise. You will be surprised, for instance, when later on, this book discusses the number of people who disappear each year.

What does this mean? Well, it means there is an ever-increasing chance that any of us, or our loved ones, could fall victim to such bizarre occurrences. None of us is "safe" under such circumstances. Moreover, if we're all at risk, then maybe we'd better know as much about what is taking place as possible. Perhaps, such knowledge may help us in some way.

Facing reality is always better than persisting in hopeful delusions to the contrary. This is because in the first instance, we can possibly then come up with answers, solutions, and/or remedies for the problem. However, if we persevere in trying to fool ourselves as to the dangers involved, we will find no such solutions or answers at all, because we refuse to believe the problem exists in the first place. In such circumstances, we would blithely continue to be the arbitrary victims of a seemingly arbitrary extraterrestrial power or powers. Under such conditions, there then might be no hope for us as individuals or as a species. Our very survival as the human race might just be what's at stake here.

This book is organized to cite examples for each aspect of the harm UFOs seem to be doing to us humans. Each type and degree of harm is categorized. In this way, I will attempt to put forth the facts on all the various types of events concerning UFOs that are a danger to us.

Again, I will cite specific instances for each category and so attempt to make my case that UFOs and their actions are not those of benevolent or even benign "space brothers," but are something far more sinister in their implications. Finally, I will attempt to draw likely conclusions as to what this means for us.

In doing this, it is my hope we will better understand the nature of UFOs, and so we will be better prepared for any eventualities with regard to them, on both a personal and national level, even world level. Even so, knowing this, we still may not be able to stop them, but going into any situation with one's eyes open is better than just blundering blindly about, flailing in every direction and to no avail.

"Knowledge is power," as "they" say and I'm a firm believer in this maxim. In the case of dealing with UFOs, extra knowledge may not give us the upper hand, or even a lot more power over our situations and predicaments with regard to UFOs, but any power is better than having none at all, or so I hope, because to be a victim is a terrible thing.

However, to be able to fight back, to any degree whatsoever, does give one a measure of hope. At least, that's my hope here, by attempting to show the true and often deadly nature of the UFO phenomenon.

This book is divided into four main parts. The first part is a general overview of the UFO phenomenon, giving background, the idea of a cover-up, the extent of it, if it exists, as well as discussing just how far those who may be perpetrating this cover-up might go.

The second part of the book delves into specific cases of being injured and killed in UFO encounters. These include both military and civilian injuries and deaths, as well as citing and discussing cases of strange deaths by UFO investigators, researchers, scientists, and journalists. This is to supply evidence for the statements made in the first section of this book.

The third part deals with the "truly bizarre," and discusses those things related to UFOs, and provides cases for those, as well. The fourth and final part of the book deals exclusively with permanent disappearances, of individuals, groups, and even entire villages. This phenomenon has been often overlooked or played down as relatively unimportant and rare. This is not the case. In fact, it may be the biggest single thing we have to fear in the whole UFO phenomenon.

Lastly, the conclusion of this book will discuss implications of such evidence, what it might mean for us all. So let us start with the Great UFO Conspiracy, as it's called, just what it entails, and what most people think it means.

So please follow along as I attempt to build a case for just why I think UFOs have such a deadly implication for us, and why the "Disappeared" enter into this all so strongly.

PART 1—THE GREAT UFO CONSPIRACY—AN OVERVIEW

"Coincidence is merely the puppeteers' curtain, hiding the hands that pull the world's strings."
—Kaleb Nation, Harken

CHAPTER 1—THE GREAT UFO CONSPIRACY THEORY

"The real rulers in Washington are invisible and exercise power from behind the scene."
—Justice Felix Frankfurter

The Great UFO Conspiracy Theory Rages On. It does so without any letup. Its adherents seem to become only more inflamed over the issues with the passing of time, as various proponents of the theory argue their cases, and their versions of the theory. To say there is a great deal of emotional baggage, passionate personal commitment, and more by many such people with regard to all this, is to make for a serious understatement.

This is because their numbers are constantly growing, and therefore, their impact on our society grows in proportion, as well. A recent survey shows this: where once the majority of Americans, just a couple of decades ago, didn't believe in the UFO phenomenon, now the majority does believe.

There are many variations on the Great UFO Conspiracy Theory and many different offshoots of it. With new events, new evidence always coming in, there is refining and adjustments to existing varieties of the conspiracy theory. People come up with new ideas almost on a daily basis, it seems.

Anyone who has watched the debate over the years can easily see this phenomenon as it progresses and evolves.

One Underlying Premise. Still, there is only the one underlying premise. This forms a bedrock foundation of beliefs uniting all of these conspiracy theories and theorists, if to greater or lesser degrees in some cases.

What is the premise? Well, its followers argue information concerning visitations by extraterrestrials or aliens, as well as the sightings of various crafts of unknown origins, "UFOs," "USOs," (Unidentified Submerged Objects) are the objects of a massive and ongoing cover-up.

Those who support this premise claim there is not only a conspiracy of silence with regard to such events and creatures appearing here on our world, but there is an active and overt attempt deliberately to suppress all information with regard to them. The adherents of this theory claim systematic and draconian methods are the tools used for this cover-up. Moreover, those who believe in the theory say people's careers and even their lives are often at stake, as with commercial airline pilots in the United States. They say these people are often too afraid of the consequences of reporting a UFO sighting for fear of losing their careers, so they simply don't.

Others claim there is massive intimidation. Finally, there are strange deaths of people involved in UFO research, as well, ones that go beyond the normal statistical range for the likelihood of such events taking place. These seem to occur, as one author on the subject put it, "in clusters."

All this, the supporters of the conspiracy say, are signs of a powerful attempt to keep the lid on the UFO phenomena, and furthermore, they say those who do this will resort to any measures, however extreme, that they feel may be necessary to achieve this goal. In short, there is nothing beyond "those" who wish to suppress the truth. They will lie, cheat, steal, intimidate, commit forgeries, or even murder to stop the idea of UFOs being taken seriously, or so conspiracy theorists say.

Now just in themselves, these are major accusations, massive and terrible ones. Together, they create probably the greatest and most far-reaching conspiracy theory ever formulated. This idea alone is enough to stretch the credulity of most people to the breaking point and beyond. To think such a massive cover-up may exist is hard to fathom.

However, it doesn't stop there. The Great UFO Conspiracy Theory goes even further. For example, it asks and then answers the question: who is doing the covering up?

The answers do vary somewhat in details, depending on which conspiracy theorist you talk to about it all. Still, it's important to remember these are just *variations on a central theme*, really just minor deviations from the main idea of who the culprit is behind the cover-up.

In short, barring some little differences in the details, most ufologists agree on the answer. There is a general and overwhelming consensus. Well then, just who is it? Who is behind this mass cover-up of all things UFO?

The answer is simple. Ask any conspiracy theorist and they will tell you those doing the covering up must be, generally and in the main, some type of human organization. Whether or not this human organization is in collusion with extraterrestrial beings is a point often argued.

Whether this is our government, other governments, a combination of them and ours, or hidden powerful group(s) within our government, so-called "shadow governments, for example, as with the supposed secret group known as Majestic Twelve, it is humans who do the covering up.

Additionally, if it is such hidden groups, then in some way they have connections to our government or multiple governments, as well, to be able to exercise the power they wield, if nothing else. Some argue, again as with the idea of the Majestic 12, that they are virtually a law unto themselves. There does seem some evidence to support this contention, but I don't want to get ahead of ourselves here.

The Great UFO Conspiracy Theory. Suffice it to say the Great UFO Conspiracy Theory holds that:

1. UFOs exist. Whether these are from Earth, another dimension, the future, or another star system, is often a subject for hot debates. The majority feel they are from somewhere else in our space, though.

2. Someone having something to do with our government(s) is responsible for the cover up.

3. The group doing this is using every method at its disposal to achieve this cover-up. This includes hiding evidence, intimidating witnesses through many means, such as the use of MIBs (those infamous "Men In Black"), outright ridicule of witnesses utilizing the media, threats to jobs and careers, mental, social, and physical intimidation, as well as even committing murders, if necessary.

4. The reason for the cover-up is unclear, but supporters insist there is one, and they have several theories as to why the cover-up exists. The purpose may be to protect the public from panic, although this theory is losing followers among the conspiracy theorists of late. Alternatively, the reason may be to hide from the public that there is a plan or goal in this conspiracy. In other words, the government and/or other entities don't want us to be aware of the UFOs, to believe in their existence, because they are planning and doing something covertly in tandem with them that they don't want us to know about for some reason.

5. What's more, this explanation furthers the idea these groups are doing all this in collusion with extraterrestrials/aliens, who may not only be aware of this conspiracy of silence with regard to the general public's knowledge of all this, but in some ways might be either instigating or actively backing such a suppression of information. Again, this would be to keep "their" goals a secret in this matter for some powerful reason. I say "powerful," because of the effort, time, and expense involved in such a massive cover-up would be incredible. Therefore, the payoff of maintaining such a silence would have to be equally profound, of great importance to whoever "they" are. UFO buffs argue the only reason to keep such a thing secret is that it is detrimental to us humans. This might be with the exception, perhaps, for a privileged few who will be granted special favor from "whoever" the services are performed. Moreover, by "whoever," they are referring to nonhuman entities.

Regardless of whether this last is true or not, many conspiracy theorists say our government is suppressing the truth about UFOs and the fact of aliens being here on our world. As mentioned earlier, various polls taken suggest the majority of Americans think the same. Specifically, a recent survey says 80 percent of Americans think the government has withheld information from them about UFOs. *(Please see references at the end of the book for a link to this data/information.)*

In other words, there is a "truth" that we are not privy to, and one which someone is actively doing their best to keep us from knowing.

If The Truth Is "Out There," Why Isn't It "Here?"
Yes, if *"the truth is out there,"* as the tagline of the television show, **X-Files**, used to say, then official organizations (albeit, secret ones, perhaps), are doing their best to keep the truth from us.

"Out there," the truth very well may be. However, those in power don't want it to be "here," to be known by all and sundry, or so the conspiracy theorists argue.

Is there any truth to these ideas of a major conspiracy and cover-up with regard to UFOs and aliens? Do others and I have credible evidence to support such extreme contentions, ones that many might even consider as just being curious and outlandish ideas, strange notions of people "not quite all there?"

What's more, if this idea of a conspiracy to suppress such knowledge is true, just how far would such organizations, whether governmental, quasi-governmental, or secret, then dare to go to keep the truth from us? Do they have any boundaries, points beyond which even they would not pass? I will attempt to answer this question later in our book, as well. Let's check out a quick list of just what UFO Conspiracy Theorists say is happening:

UFOs Injure People. UFOs have injured many. Observers of these strange craft can end up by suffering from bizarre maladies, long-term illnesses that haunt them the rest of their shortened lives. The number of such incidents, injuries, illnesses, and deaths are far higher than the average person realizes. What's more, they have been going on for far longer than one would think, meaning centuries, even millennia, or possibly even longer. This is not even counting the emotional and psychological injuries people have suffered in the thousands from their close encounters with alien spacecraft. We're strictly talking literal, physical injuries here.

Yet for some strange reason, which I will get into later in this book, few seem to know about this aspect of UFO encounters. Alternatively, if they do, they are only aware of a very limited number of such instances and so think them a rare occurrence.

The result of this? Well, most tend to think these deaths and injuries aren't particularly significant. They are just "an exceptional event." In other words, when these unfortunate things take place, they are just an unusual "accident."

In addition, accidents do happen, as they say. Right? In other words, "our space brothers" didn't' mean to do that, commit those terrible atrocities. They were just tragic mistakes and rare ones, at that.

Well, are they? Are such dreadful outcomes of humans having contact with UFOs and their occupants just a series of luckless mishaps? If so, these mishaps repeat on a regular basis. What's more, they can and sometimes do have deadly consequences for those involved.

Abductions. There is more. People now in the *millions* claim abductions by the occupants of UFOs, and had painful and intrusive experiments performed on them, strange devices inserted into them during such abductions and experiments, as well as having permanent implants injected into them. Many swear they repeatedly are the victims of alien abductions or such kidnappings.

In addition, they usually stress the experiments are akin to a form of torture of the most brutal and painful sort. Are all these just accidents, too? Don't our alien "space brothers" know better, know they are inflicting intense pain upon all these people they abduct? It would seem unlikely they could be so ignorant of the torment they cause.

Sadly, this sort of thing is nothing new. What the average person may not know is just how far back reports of these sorts of abductions go. Claims of this, of seeing UFOs and then having missing time are nothing new in history.

For instance, the first such reported incident on the North American Continent was in 1639, the better part of 400 years ago! This occurred on the Charles River in Colonial Boston. The Charles River Incident involved several men in a boat who saw a bright, "pig-shaped" light in the sky and then couldn't account for several hours of their time. In short, they had the infamous "missing time" which so many abduction cases have. In Europe, abduction reports go back even farther in time.

Animal Mutilations. Yet, there is even still more. I have researched reports, worldwide and not just in North America, of literally thousands of strange animal mutilations, truly bizarre ones. These often seem to have no rational explanation and are not the result of "natural causes," or "natural predation," meaning they aren't the result of attacks by other animals. Often, UFO sightings occur in the area where and when these happen.

Crop Circles, "The Devil's Tramping Ground. The same holds true for the crop circle phenomenon. In addition, if you think these are all just hoaxes in their thousands, think again. Such circles have existed throughout our history, frightened many people over the centuries. They have been variously referred to as "Devil's Circles," "Devil's Tramping Ground," as with the one in North Carolina near Siler City, "Fairy Rings" (not to be confused with the circular growth of fungi and mushrooms), and more! This means that if all crop circles now are only modern day hoaxes, then they have ancient roots in reality.

Mind you, in the Middle Ages, anyone caught doing such a thing as creating crop circles in the middle of the night as a practical joke or hoax would have been summarily accused of witchcraft, tried as a witch, and then burned, drowned, or killed in some other deplorable and agonizing manner. So the idea, people would commit such hoaxes back then just for fun, with such enormous consequences, just doesn't seem too likely.

So today, although many crop circles could well be hoaxes, the sheer number, size, and intricacy of some makes it equally unlikely that all are. Some are so complex, so huge, that estimates say it would take tens of people more time than one night would allow for them to complete such tasks. The upshot? Some crop circles are not hoaxes. However, if not, what are they?

Individuals Disappear. This is a subject the book will discuss at some length later on, because it is one of the strangest, and perhaps most frightening of all aspects of the UFO phenomenon. The "Disappeared" aren't just alien abductions in the modern or usual sense of the idea, where people are kidnapped, experimented on, and then returned. Rather, people disappear permanently and under truly uncanny circumstances. More often than not, these defy logical explanations, at least of the ordinary variety.

Moreover, if you think this is a rare occurrence, think again! As discussed later in this book, disappearances of people have occurred throughout history and under the strangest of circumstances, sometimes occurring right in front of the eyes of multiple witnesses in broad daylight.

Whole Villages Disappear. Not just individuals disappear. Therefore, it's not just the "rare few" disappearing. Because, you see, reports of the entire populations of villages vanishing, never to be seen again, with no remains later found, do keep happening. This has incredible implications. These, too, date back far into our history.

Therefore, whether it's the entire crews of ships, individuals "going out for a package of cigarettes and never returning home," or whole villages of people vanishing never to be seen again, this is a constant and recurring phenomenon, the so-called "Disappeared." It would also appear to be a deadly one for those involved, since once gone, they seem to be gone forever.

We must ask the question: just what is going on here? People in their thousands, even millions, have endured hardships, illness, and death. Loved ones have vanished forever and this has happened repeatedly. Strange sightings fill our skies now more than ever. The number of UFO sightings worldwide climbs with each passing year.

So is there a connection to all these things? Yes, there does seem to be, but just what the connection entails, what it means for us, and our futures, is something that should be given much more attention to now than it has been in the past, since the phenomena seems to be steadily growing in size and number of incidents.

We must consider certain things. Where most writers focus on individual events, feeling the more evidence they produce of such things occurring, the more people will realize there is actually a problem "out there," I want to focus more on trends. My interest is more in the overall results of what others and I are seeing happen, because this is important for us all.

CHAPTER 2—EXTENT OF THE COVERUP?

"Secrecy is the beginning of tyranny."
—**Author Robert Heinlein**

How Far Will "They" Go? If there is an actual conspiracy to cover up the whole UFO phenomenon in all its guises, as mentioned in Chapter 1, and there seems to be, then the question has to be asked: just how far would they go to maintain such a thing? Many others ask this question, as well.

For example, would they, whoever precisely "they" are, truly go so far as to ruin reputations and careers? Is any tactic then within their range of use? Would they really alter evidence? Would they cause those who report such events to become the object of deliberately induced ridicule, for example?

We can go further with such questions. For example, would they, as a number of ufologists claim, even resort to assassinating individuals in order to shut them up? Are they capable of coldblooded murder to achieve their goals of ruthless suppression of all things UFO and extraterrestrial? If so, why? What is so important that it is worth murdering people to keep secret?

To say the very least, these are disturbing questions. To cover up something for fear of causing a general panic is one thing and bad enough, especially if it means lying, distorting the truth, coming up with phony "explanations" that are the stuff of nonsense when closely examined. Lies are lies, no matter how one looks at it. Therefore, to tell one, there should be a very good reason for doing so, and the word "good" is the operative word here. However, this does not seem to be the case in reality, as this book will show.

Even if there were such a good reason, to destroy careers, people's livelihoods and lives, and even commit murder, is something else quite again. On the one hand, one could argue the government is acting as if it were some sort of benign and paternalistic dictatorship, trying to do what it thinks is best for us all.

Admittedly, this would be at the expense of the comparative few and their careers or lives, but done so for the sake of the wellbeing of the majority of us. To put it in other words, they, the government, just want to preserve law and order. They want to allow most, if not all of us, to continue our lives in relatively uninterrupted peace by using an ongoing process of denial and cover-up.

On the other hand, if they go further, if the government or "someone" is actually physically intimidating people, threatening their lives, menacing them with imprisonment, and/or actually killing them, then this is quite a different matter entirely. This would be a gross violation of the very law and order they would be claiming to protect, especially, if they resort to murdering people and/or permanently destroying their reputations. They would be committing the most basic violations of our Constitutional and human rights.

If this is so, if this is happening, what then? Could such extreme measures ever be justified under any circumstances? Moreover, has this actually happened or is the whole idea just one of those *outré* conspiracy theories, and a truly "crazy" notion, at that?

Well, there seems to be real evidence some of this sort of thing might well have occurred, and is continuing to occur, and much more often than just once or twice. In fact, it seems such extreme measures might have occurred many times over and to many different people. The tactics of destroying or altering evidence, suppression of facts, and intimidation of people does seem to be a very real thing.

If this is indeed so, then this is unconscionable, should not be allowed, and should be stopped. The price to maintain law and order should not be the constant and severe breaking of those same laws, of resorting to the deliberate destruction of people's lives and even the taking of some of those lives.

The government does seem to try to cover up things in other ways besides these, as well. If someone's statements of evidence seem incontrovertible and they are very high-profile persons, another tactic used by the "powers-that-be" is to attack the credibility of the witness by literally making them a "non-person." As we will see later on, this is just what happens to some.

However, in some cases, as with John Murphy of the Kecksburg Incident in Pennsylvania, he is made first into a non-person and then he ends up dead. Of course, all these statements here would be baseless if there was no proof of such types of threats and intimidations. Yet, we do have such proof. For instance:

Deathbed Confession. This is one of the most compelling proofs there is an ongoing cover-up by the federal government of the whole UFO phenomenon. However, let's start at the beginning, and yes, you've heard part of this story before, at least, but perhaps not how it all ended and that was with a bang instead of a whimper. First, a brief recapitulation of events, just to make the matter fresh in our minds:

July 2, 1947, media reported a UFO or "flying disc" as having crashed near Roswell, New Mexico. The official press release at the time of the occurrence stated:

"The many rumors regarding the flying disc became a reality yesterday when the intelligence officer of the 509th Bomb Group of the Eighth Air Force, Roswell Army Air Field, was fortunate enough to gain possession of a disc."

This, on the face of it, would seem very cut and dried. Moreover, the announcement resulted in a wave of dramatic newspaper headlines across the United States and elsewhere, such as, *"Flying Disc captured by Air Force."*

To say the reaction to these headlines was immediate and impressive is seriously to understate the situation of the times. Furthermore, this incident began the whole idea of a UFO cover-up by the federal government. This is with good reason, I feel, because of the events that followed the announcement and those incredible headlines.

For example, just one day after the announcement and as most of us already know, the military authorities entirely reversed what they had to say, and as just about everyone now also knows, claimed the event was really just a crashed weather balloon that had been mistaken by the officer in charge as a "flying disc."

To add to this tale, an officer was forced to squat by the wreckage of a balloon. He then had his picture taken to prove the military's revised version of events was true. This, the officer did. Although in retrospect, it must have been an incredibly humiliating thing for him to do, and no doubt, destroyed his career in the military as a result. In essence, he was "taking the fall," to help dismiss the notion of a wrecked UFO having actually been recovered.

One of the astonishing things about all this was how quickly journalists and their publishers accepted this complete turnaround, and virtually without question, or a murmur. Of course, we must remember that at the time, the American people largely still believed wholeheartedly the government always told them the truth. Not so much, these days, it seems and with good reason, I think. In any case, this seemed to have put the whole Roswell matter at rest for the time being.

However, time marched on and things began to change in this regard. People began to question the government's revised version of events, as one by one, witnesses to various things surrounding the Roswell crash began to step forward and recount what they had seen, heard, and experienced at the time the crash took place. Moreover, we must remember, there actually was a crash of "something." Even the government has never denied that. In any case, this caused doubt to creep in about the government's "weather balloon" explanation. More and more people began to question the whole thing.

Erosion of the credibility of the government's tale continued when Major Jesse Marcel, an officer who had gone in person to the crash site, and eventually "came out" to describe in detail the nature of some of the wreckage as being not of this Earth. If he is to be believed, the materials found out there in the desert could not have been from an American weather balloon or anything else native to this world.

Therefore, the controversy raged on about Roswell and what actually took place there. During this prolonged period, the government changed its story about the event with regard to the "weather balloon" several times. Instead of reassuring the public by doing this, the government further undermined its credibility with the American people.

After all, how many "revisions" could the public be expected to believe, and which version was the true one, and which ones were the lies? That the government changed its story about Roswell several times is a matter of public record. That this diminished the average person's belief in the idea the government was telling the truth is also a matter of record. Polls indicated a steady erosion of trust in the government, as well as what they told the public as being "true."

Then something very profound happened and this is the reason I've recounted the Roswell Incident here. This event was so astonishing, as to make even diehard skeptics reconsider whether or not a UFO had crashed at Roswell.

It amounts to nothing less than a full-fledged, deathbed confession.

Walter Haut, at the time of the Roswell incident, was a lieutenant, and had been in charge of all public relations concerning the event, at least, initially. Haut, it seemed, had seen the wreckage of the alien spacecraft, had told another (and at this point, it was just hearsay) that he had actually seen an alien body, as well.

This was according to an interview with Lt. Richard Harris, Jr. He was in the base's financial department, and had worked there when these events were supposed to have occurred. So on the face of it, such a statement could have been true, since both men worked their together at the same time, 1947. However, again, at the time this was just said by Harris. This means it was still just hearsay and unsubstantiated by Haut, himself, with regard to the dead body of an alien. These remarks attributed to him were by third-party investigators. Therefore, of course, they had to be taken with the proverbial grain of salt.

It was further said that Huat had been intimately involved with many details of the UFO event, since he had been placed in charge of all press releases from that point forward by Colonel William Blanchard. It would seem Haut was one of the original "spin doctors" in this regard.

Yet, when interviewed in later decades, long years after the Roswell incident occurred, and despite still being highly circumspect about what he had to say, Haut is said to have ended his interviews in many cases, with the following statement, quote: *"It wasn't any type of weather balloon. I believe it was a UFO! Just don't ask me why!"*

Still, despite such telling and leading comments, what Haut may have actually seen or not seen, remained something of a real mystery. That is, until he died. Walter Haut passed away in December of 2005. It turns out; the man had made a sworn affidavit before his death with reference to the Roswell UFO incident and its aftermath.

In his testimony, sworn, witnessed and notarized, he said the assertions by the military the UFO had in reality just been a weather balloon had been utterly false. He further stated the UFO had been seized by the military/government and secreted at another base in a hangar there. However, in his statement, although he did describe the alien vessel, or rather, the remnants of it, he concentrated more on the fact of having seen alien bodies.

He wasn't the only one to have talked of such bodies. Various people, including a Roswell undertaker (Glenn Dennis) stated he had to provide coffins designed for children to the military. He claimed a nurse at the base also mentioned alien bodies.

Some of the highpoints of Haut's testimony include:

- A secret meeting which included General Roger Ramey, who at the time was the Eighth Army Commander, as well as Colonel William Blanchard, and others.

- Parts from the crashed UFO were examined, although nobody was able to identify of what the materials consisted.

- A second crash site had also been located, and this was the better one, contained more things of interest. This was the primary location of importance.

- The first crash site, with the weather balloon story, made for a convenient cover-up of the second and more important crash site.

- There was to be a full cleansing of both sites, with no evidence left for anyone to find and/or stumble upon later. It would be as if nothing of importance had ever happened there. This would include any "souvenirs" or pieces of wreckage local inhabitants of the region might have already taken from the site. These were to be tracked down and then summarily confiscated.

- Haut also claims the colonel took him to view the wreckage, which seemed in remarkable condition, despite the crash, being "egg-shaped," about 12 to 15 feet long and approximately 6 feet wide. There were no outstanding features other than this.

- Haut also claims in his affidavit that he saw two bodies, ones with tarps covering part of them. In addition, as with all the descriptions we've heard about over the decades, the alien crewmembers were about 4 feet in length and had huge heads.

- Haut also states in the affidavit that he was thoroughly convinced these were creatures not of this Earth. His exact statement was, *"I am convinced that what I personally observed was some kind of craft and its crew from outer space."*

It is important to remember here that during his life, Walter Haut never mentioned he saw alien bodies or an alien spacecraft, at least not in public. He remained quiet about this for his entire life, although, as mentioned above, he did often allude to the fact there was more to the whole Roswell event than he was willing or allowed to divulge.

It was as if having kept the word of his oath, he was, in his own way, trying to violate the spirit of it in the sense of trying to impart more information to people, but without technically violating his oath of secrecy in the process. Of course, upon his death, as with all things of this world, his promises and oaths were no longer of force and effect. He was free to say what he wanted to, if only posthumously.

Let's be absolutely clear here; to sign a notarized and duly witnessed affidavit prior to his death, at the time having been certified to be in good mental health, and the statement only to be released to the public after his death, is a very telling point. The affidavit was not only his sworn testimony on the Roswell Incident, but also, for all practical purposes, constituted a deathbed confession of what he knew, of what really had gone on with regard to Roswell.

Why did he do this? Well, one might argue he was doing an elaborate practical joke, one he was perpetrating from "beyond the grave," as it were. However, nobody who knew William Haut would think or believe such a thing. Nothing in his entire life indicated he would contrive to such a hoax.

Furthermore, when people "are facing their maker," as the adage goes, most want to pass from this world with a clean conscience. The fact he was willing to sign such an affidavit in front of family and witnesses, have it notarized, would seem to indicate this was his intent—to have a clear conscience when he died. It was, in every sense of the word, his deathbed confession, therefore.

Why didn't Haut come forth before he died? Well, the consequences to himself and those close to him could have been devastating. This was during the height of the Cold War. Anyone, especially a military officer, divulging anything considered a matter of national security, and having sworn not to do so, was guilty of a whole range of crimes. This included, but was not limited to high treason.

The consequences of his having divulged such a secret would have not been a good thing for him or those he loved. This is especially true when in retrospect; there have been so many claims of intimidation, threats on the lives of other witnesses involved in this event, as well as others.

What do I believe? I believe William Haut told the truth, that the affidavit was a real deathbed confession, and that the man had no reason to lie or alter the facts. He told us what he believed to be true. So yes, there does seem to have been a major cover-up of the whole UFO phenomenon practically from the outset.

As another side note, a military man, Colonel Philip Corso, also claimed to have had access to some of the alien artifacts, claiming it was his job to disseminate the materials for investigation by various agencies, including private corporations of the time. His death of heart failure so soon after divulging this information only seems to add fuel to the fire of conspiracy theories charging the government resorts to murders (covered up ones, of course, those made to look "natural" or as just "accidents"). If not, perhaps he knew his health was bad and had just decided it was time to come forward with what he knew before he faced his demise.

Neither is this claim of Corso's unsubstantiated. Others, including the one-time Minister of Defense for Canada, say they heard corroborating statements from other sources that what Corso said was, in fact, true.

Furthermore, the behavior of the government with regard to all this casts even further doubt about their veracity in the matter. At the time, they claimed it was just a weather balloon. Later, in the '90's, they claimed it was a cover-up to hide a high altitude test referred to as Project Mogul, but had nothing to do with UFOs. Then even later, 1997, another report said the so-called aliens had just been dummies for the test flight.

Yes, the story kept changing over the years to the point where the government's credibility in this matter seems almost nonexistent now. Why change the story so often if true? Why keep adding to it, modifying it, as if to better fit the circumstances of what had been reported initially? Why not just take one story and stick with it?

Well, the answer to that is obvious; hardly anyone believed it; not then, not later, and not now. So in an attempt to calm troubled waters, it would seem the government kept modifying the account of what had been discovered to try to incorporate what had been stated by others, various witnesses, and to "disarm" the skeptics with not-so-clever attempts to supply alternate answers.

If there is no conspiracy, if there is nothing hide, if no UFOs exist, why these attempts to cover-up something, when there is supposedly nothing to cover-up? It does make one wonder...

Furthermore, even foreign governments are convinced that our government is involved in a conspiracy to cover up the whole phenomenon of UFOs. For instance, an official report published by the government of France, titled: *UFOs and Defense: What Must We Be Prepared For?* in 1999, stated quite clearly that our (US) government was withholding "valuable" evidence with regard to the whole UFO topic and/or the threat such craft might imply for all.

Nor does it stop there with regard to formal accusations of cover-ups. For instance, there is dependable testimony the Technical Intelligence Division at Wright-Patterson and Project Sign, made an official and so-called "Estimate of the Situation." This was in 1948. At the time, the Estimate was classified, included sightings of UFOs by very reliable witnesses (scientists, pilots, etc.). The Estimate finished by saying not only that there were UFOs, but they were not of this Earth.

CONCLUSION. Even all this evidence aside, reverse logic alone gives us the answer about the idea of whether UFOs exist or not, because if there is a definite cover-up going on, then there must be something to cover up. It's as simple as that.

Furthermore, with the evidence for a cover-up as shown above being real, and there is much, much more where that came from, one can invoke this reverse logic to show there really must be UFOs, because of the ongoing cover-up about them, and that cover-up being of such major proportions.

How much does it take before we are to be convinced? If a deathbed confession of a United States military officer, one who was intimately involved in the whole Roswell event, one good enough to have security clearances, and who gave testimony that was witnessed, signed, and notarized, is not enough to convince one, then probably nothing could.

This is the case with some people and it runs the entire spectrum. There are those who require little evidence to believe something is true (not a good thing), those who require more evidence to arrive at the same conclusion, but there are also those who will refuse to believe no matter how much evidence is supplied. This may well be out of fear, fear of the unknown, fear that their view of reality isn't what they want it to be, so denial of UFOs is easier than dealing with them.

Moreover, the idea that *"extraordinary evidence must be supplied to support extraordinary claims,"* as Carl Sagan said, is great in principle, but not in fact. Because, you see, there is the problem of who decides what such *"extraordinary evidence"* is. The scientists who would accept such evidence are themselves the self-appointed arbiters of what constitutes *"extraordinary evidence."* This mean, they alone decide what's "good enough" to be admissible as such to them. It's a bit like the police policing themselves. They can dismiss whatever they choose out of hand, as a result.

Apparently, they do, because the testimony of police officers, pilots—both military and commercial, military personnel at bases, and millions of people worldwide doesn't constitute sufficient evidence for these scientists to investigate the matter. Neither do the countless photographs or videos taken seem even to hold much sway with them. The recordings of radar showing such UFO intrusions, or the carefully compiled fieldwork by trained MUFON Field Investigators for decades now, is not enough either. Short of delivering a UFO to such "objective" scientists, it's hard to imagine what else may constitute a piece of evidence *"extraordinary"* enough to appease their arbitrary hurdles as to what is acceptable evidence.

What does this mean for the whole UFO phenomenon that scientists feel or behave this way with regard to them? Well, two things are immediate repercussions of such behavior. The first is that such a negative attitude about accepting bona fide evidence of the sort mentioned above, acts as another, if inadvertent conspiracy to cover-up the whole UFO question. If scientists, as a group, refuse even to consider the idea, then this is aiding those who are conspiring to cover up the whole thing.

The second point here is scientists may simply not have a choice in refusing to consider evidence, their not wanting to investigate UFOs. As we've mentioned in other books, to do so is a dangerous thing for most scientists and researchers' careers.

Their work can depend heavily on grants from the government in the form of both private grants and public ones, such as to universities. These grants can and do dry up if the government chooses for them to do so, and so such researchers, dependent on such funds, must dance to the tune of our government or lose that obligatory funding of their research.

They must not only work on what interests the government, but they must **not** work on that which doesn't. Or more pointedly said, they couldn't work on that which the government forbids them to, at least, not without severe repercussions for their careers.

The result is, whether inadvertently or not, by not investigating the whole UFO question, scientists are aiding in the conspiracy of silence on this matter.

There is something else in this regard, as well, and this, too, makes it hard to challenge the conspiracy of silence and/or cover-up of UFOs. As always in this world, some simply refuse to be convinced, no matter what. As mentioned above, fear isn't the only reason for this. Nobody likes their world viewpoint challenged, especially when the challenge is in the form of something as frightening as the subject of the existence of UFOs.

So for some, the ostrich-burying-its-head-in-the-sand syndrome kicks in, and nothing and no one can persuade such people to believe or think otherwise. In a way, they are to be envied, for they can steadfastly refuse and refute all the evidence shown to them to the contrary, and so continue to live in their safe little world, and no matter what. However, I feel this world of theirs, sadly, is more one of wishful thinking, of their imagination, than it is a reality. We live in a harsh reality and to retreat into the idea we can have security is simply wrong, because security is an illusion. There really is no such thing.

Finally, it must be said that for the scientific community to ignore the whole question of UFOs is strange in another way. Why? Well, even if UFOs aren't real, their huge impact on society, not just ours but around the world, constitutes a real and powerful social phenomenon. Why wouldn't scientists want to explore this facet of the whole UFO question, at least?

If more than half of all Americans, for example, believe in UFOs, but they don't exist, then wouldn't scientists want to investigate just why this is so? If nothing else, it would seem to make for an interesting question for sociologists and psychologists to want to explore. But…nothing!

No research group of any consequence is endeavoring to explore this strange social phenomenon. Yes, there are a few independent researchers curious enough, the odd psychologist, but no large-scale funding of mainstream research exists to pursue this question as to why so many people, in the hundreds of millions, would insist on believing something scientists say just doesn't exist? They explore just about every other social phenomenon, writing reams of dissertations on sex, religion, various other social proclivities, but not the fact that the majority of Americans believe in UFOs? Really? This seems very strange…one has to ask, why not?

CHAPTER 3—HOW FAR WOULD OUR GOVERNMENT GO?

"The issue today is the same as it has been throughout all history, whether man shall be allowed to govern himself or be ruled by a small elite."
—Thomas Jefferson

Would our government really go so far as to murder its own citizens? Moreover, if they wouldn't stop there, exactly, where would they stop? Is there any line in the sand they would not cross, not dare to go beyond if this is the case? Would there be any limits at all, to what they would not resort to, in order to achieve their goals of silence and suppression?

One needs answers as well, to other questions. As just one instance, if the majority of Americans believe UFOs already exist, and again, polls indicate this is the case, then why such a massive effort to suppress the fact of their existence at this point? Why bother?

Isn't it rather like the old saying of "closing the barn door after all the cattle are out?" If most of us now believe UFOs are real, why bother to go to such extreme efforts to hide this fact at this late date?

Is it just out of an ingrained habit on the government's part at this point, some sort of ossified bureaucracy that isn't keeping pace with the times and is incapable of staying abreast of public sentiment? Alternatively, is there still more to all this we don't know about, something of a sinister nature, perhaps? Maybe, admitting to the existence of UFOs and/or extraterrestrials is just the tip of an iceberg, and one about which the government doesn't want us to know?

What Secret Is Still Unknown To Us About All This? What terrible hidden part of this, what top-secret thing still unknown to the populace would cause our government to go to such lengths, such extreme measures to resort to maintaining the cover-up? When UFOs are seen in such massive numbers, over a million sightings a year worldwide, why the constant attempt to explain away such sightings as just mundane events? This does seem to be just what they are doing, and on many levels of government.

2006, UFO Sighted Over O'Hare International Airport In Chicago. A number of airline employees watched what appeared to be a UFO directly above the airport. They witnessed this for a considerable amount of time. They became concerned and reported the event. Eventually, the UFO shot straight upwards, *"punching a hole in the clouds"* as it was described, and so leaving a noticeable circular gap in the cloud layer there. Not only did members of the maintenance crew for the airline witness this event, but also so did many passengers waiting to board flights, as well as just some passersby. We're talking well over a hundred people at the minimum. They even took photos. Yet, no formal investigation was conducted taken or completed!

FAA Ignores Official Requests For Investigation. However, multiple requests were made for the FAA to investigate the matter. Their response was they would not, that this was just a misunderstood weather event. (Sounds so similar to the old excuse of a "weather balloon," or "swamp gas," doesn't it?) Therefore, it didn't need any investigation, at least as far as the FAA was concerned.

This is a very strange response by the FAA, no matter how one tries to perceive it. Remember, this took place at one of the world's busiest airports, in the air right above it, and therefore, such an unexplained event could have repercussions for the safety of airline travelers, and jets, even if it were just an unusual weather event.

The FAA is charged with investigating anything out of the ordinary involving commercial air flights and/or airports. It is ***their job*** to investigate anything that in any way may constitute a danger, or possible danger to air traffic. The fact multiple witnesses were involved, photographs taken, and several requests for investigations made, should have been more than sufficient grounds for the FAA to have some concern and so officially probe the matter.

They didn't. They did nothing at all. How could the FAA be sure it was just a weather event without such an investigation taking place in the first place to confirm this explanation? So why wouldn't the FAA explore the incident as a matter of course, if only just to find out, one way or the other, if what was witnessed posed any sort of threat? Again, they did not. Yet, what happened was significant enough to make the local and national news!

Once more, why didn't the FAA investigate this matter? Again, this is their job, after all. This is one of the main reasons for their existence. This is supposed to be exactly what they are to do under such peculiar circumstances. So yet again, one has to ask, why didn't they? Why did they just ignore the whole thing as if it never happened at all?

So one can see there are many questions about this response by the FAA. There is even more involved here, much more. The government or *someone* doesn't just seem to be resorting to ignoring or refusing to investigate such things. It seems they might be going even farther.

Deaths Of UFO Witnesses. Why is this of significance? Well, as mentioned, there have been deaths, too. There have been quite a number of them.

For some reason, even those delving deeply into the subject of UFOs don't talk about these types of incidents much, at least not until recently. For a long time, even people who spoke about all things UFO didn't discuss these occurrences to any real extent. It is almost as if there was a conspiracy of silence in this regard, too, and even among those willing to discuss everything else about UFOs.

That is, until relatively recently. News about these fatal events is finally coming out via the Internet and television, and so, too, in books, such as this one. The seeming conspiracy of silence in this regard seems to have at last faltered and begun to fail.

However, there are those who say such deaths and injuries are not something of any real consequence, except perhaps, to those who are injured or killed, and their relatives, it would seem. One would think this was consequence enough, just in itself.

Many of this persuasion argue such things just happen by accident, but are not deliberate. After all, given enough encounters with UFOs by enough people, by sheer chance some would go terribly wrong. Right? Alien craft appear in our skies so often that the occasional injuries and deaths would result at times, just by sheer bad chance. Does this argument really hold water? Well, the best way to decide this is to make a quick example of how this could be with a brief scenario.

Comparison Scenario. Let's consider the following scenario: Advanced Europeans arrive in the New World. They quickly build a train track, one upon which a train occasionally runs, but not necessarily at regular intervals, perhaps only when needed. Some Native Americans see the locomotive go by from a great distance and for the first time. Others see it close-up, right by the tracks. Some see it going away from them, while others see it coming right toward them. Sometimes, it is only one person who spots the train, and other times it's a group. Some of the sightings are in daylight, and others are at night, where the train is just a dark shape with lights moving across the landscape.

To continue the scenario, once in a great while, a Native American strays onto the track at just the wrong moment and is killed or injured by the train. In other words, there was an accident involved in witnessing the train go by, but one where there was no real intent to kill or harm anyone. It was just an accident and nothing more.

This scenario could be used to argue the same thing is happening with UFOs. UFOs could be like the locomotive. Moreover, we can take the scenario even a step further, to explain why people see different types of UFOs.

For instance, the Native Americans could be compared to UFO witnesses. Descriptions of the locomotive, as told by the Native Americans, would vary greatly, depending on where, when, and how they chanced to see the locomotive. Same train, but with very different descriptions, since some natives would describe a weird light floating by in the darkness to the accompaniment of strange noises, while others would describe a large long object belching smoke and thundering across the plains in broad daylight. The exact same thing could be applied to modern UFO witnesses. Witnesses would see them under different conditions, as well, at different distances, in different lighting, etc.

On the face of it, this is a reasonable comparison scenario to UFO sightings and one that could readily apply to the whole UFO question. It would resolve the issue of such sightings, injuries, and/or deaths. They are just the occasional accident, just as that hypothetical locomotive might kill the occasional Native American.

Nevertheless, is this the actual case? Does this scenario really apply to explain such occurrences and really hold up with regard to UFOs?

Problems With Scenario. The problem is that unlike with the train in our scenario, which is on tracks, and so can't go out of its way to hurt or kill people, sometimes, UFOs seem to be doing exactly this. Individuals seem to be "marked," as it were, and singled out as targets.

On occasion, this results in their injuries, long-term illnesses, and/or even death. So how can these events be considered just accidents if this is so? They can't be. This can't be so, not when the people involved are seemingly "hunted" by the UFOs, chased down by them at times, and then wounded or killed by them.

Therefore, whatever is going on isn't quite as simple as our initial comparison scenario would have us believe. Yes, like the train scenario, people are being injured in UFO encounters. People are dying. However, in some cases, this seems to be on deadly purpose by the UFOs/aliens. Trains don't deliberately leave the tracks and chase people with such deadly intent, sometimes for long minutes at a time, in order to injure or kill them. Whereas, UFOs have been reported to do just this. In other words, some of the deaths involving UFO encounters do not seem to be accidents.

One can go even further with our comparison. Unlike with accidental train deaths of our Native Americans in our fictitious scenario, which would certainly be bad enough, nobody would go about the countryside intimidating witnesses to such events, force them into silence about the fact of the "accident," or force any such witnesses to recant their testimonies.

However, repeatedly, witnesses of UFO occurrences often report just this sort of thing, with "official-like" individuals, the so-called infamous "Men in Black" coming to intimidate them into silence about what they'd seen. This would seem to show the deaths and/or injuries, as well as the witnessing of such events, are subject to a deliberate and systematic suppression. Why?

So common is the concept of the mysterious Men in Black, several movies have been made on the subject. Yes, they were done as comedies. To do otherwise might just not have been a good idea for the health and wellbeing of the producers and directors, given the circumstances…given that people are subject to public denigration, ridicule, and being made into non-persons.

Again, there might be a deliberate attempt to ridicule the whole idea of the concept of Men in Black, by making outlandish and comedic movies about them. Always, there seems, there is this element of ridicule invoked or involved. It is an attempt to make it a group/public consensus that such ideas are strictly comical and farcical, that only the "fringe element" would believe such things.

In other words, can't make "it" (meaning UFO sightings) go away? Then resort to ridicule by having people make comedy movies and shows of it. If it works with airplane pilots, civilian professionals, and military personnel, it should work just as well for those witnesses who claim such intimidation by mysterious strangers dressed in black suits.

In addition, let's be honest here. Whenever anyone dares even to mention having seen something strange in the way of a UFO, they often preface their statement with some like, "I don't want you to think I'm crazy, or some kind of nut, but…"

This, in itself, tells us a lot. Anyone who even dares legitimately to voice what they saw, whatever it might have been, has to first disavow the idea they are insane to dare do it! This is why so many people simply don't report such events. It's just safer for them and their reputations not to do this.

Deaths Of UFO Researchers. With this whole topic of death and injuries, there is something else, something even more frightening to consider, as well. Not only are people being injured or killed in some UFO incidents, but so are those who investigate the incidents after they've already occurred! Remember, these people aren't dying in UFO accidents, themselves, but in other ways, some markedly mysterious and strange ones, while conducting their investigations, or after having done so.

Somebody seems to be doing actual killings or assassinations of some of these UFO researchers and investigators. Just who is doing this, if this is true, and why? Whatever the answers to these questions are, there does seem to be a definite pattern of this sort of thing actually taking place. There is evidence of pattern s of "clusters" of deaths in this regard, which we will go into in far more depth later on this book, in Part 2.

Are these just quirky incidents, and nothing more? It would seem this is definitely not the case. The circumstances, numbers, and connections of the people dying seem to defy the idea of the deaths being just random events and unrelated. They appear to be something far more sinister.

Again, why? Why would anyone resort to such extreme measures? Wouldn't the deaths in themselves raise even more suspicions? If so, then why commit such murders? Is it as a last resort, in order to shut people up who won't be silenced in any other way? It could be. On the other hand, perhaps it is because certain researchers are getting dangerously close to finding certain truths? That could be, as well.

One thing does seem self-evident. If people are being murdered to silence them, if "someone" is willing to go to such lengths to shut them up permanently, then whatever the secret is they are trying to hide must be a monumental one and worth hiding from the public. Again, with the majority of Americans now believing UFOs are real, the secret can't be something as banal as just pretending still that they aren't real. After all, at this point, the battle in that regard already seems to be lost.

No, whatever the reason for these deaths, it is to hide a much bigger secret than that. Something major is at stake here. It's something that some are willing to keep secret at any cost, even at the ultimate price of committing murders. By that very reasoning, the secret would seem to have very dark connotations.

One can see there are a lot of questions that need answering and quickly, because if this is going on, it constitutes a major danger for many, in fact, anyone who might witness UFOs, or then starting real, in-depth inquiries into them.

Just to be clear at this point, I feel there is one question that doesn't need answering. That question is, "Do UFOs really exist?"

I've already answered this in other books I've written and shown much evidence to support the fact of their existence, but I will reiterate my opinion here for those who may not have read any of them.

UFOs do exist. I feel there is a massive preponderance of evidence for their existence. If over a million sightings occur every year, and worldwide, and only five percent of those are actual sightings and not something misconstrued as being UFOs, just as experts/skeptics say, then obviously UFOs do exist. Five percent, even as the skeptics insist (but probably more), are seeing something real and very strange. Ergo, UFOs exist. There are bona fide Unidentified Flying Objects in our skies, ones that simply can't be accounted for as some form of our own aircraft, military or otherwise, or some natural phenomenon.

What's more, I insist upon this fact. Why? Well, because of simple math. If only five percent are actual sightings of UFOs, then that still leaves approximately **50,000 or more sightings a year that are genuine!** These sightings can't be accounted for any other way. Moreover, these are where people are seeing something extraordinary and by that, I literally mean "extra-ordinary."

Since this has been going on for decades, even centuries, and perhaps thousands of years, there is no doubt UFOs exist. The evidence is in. The facts are conclusive. We all have to deal with it.

Something Is Going On With UFOs. Moreover, I feel something is definitely going on, that the UFOs/extraterrestrials have an agenda, if you will. Too much evidence indicates too often that UFOs are seen around military bases, have interfered with nuclear launching capabilities, have buzzed and or even landed near such bases, as well as seemingly tempting our air forces (not just the American one), to attempt to engage them.

If these are just meant as demonstrations of the UFOs' capabilities, it seems they have more than sufficiently demonstrated this and many times over. No, something more than just mere examples of their power and capabilities are going on here. Although, that may well be a big part of it. After this overview section, I will delve deeper into this matter, as well.

Strange Deaths And Disappearances Of Innocents. Besides researchers of UFO phenomena experiencing strange deaths after the fact, there have been UFO-related deaths and disappearances of witnesses of such events during the actual occurrences, as well. These are far more widespread than you may realize. They have occurred all over the globe. For instance, entire villages have disappeared. Individuals have vanished in mid-step and in plain sight of multiple witnesses. People in groups have died under mysterious circumstances where UFOs have been recently sighted.

These people range from hikers, to family members driving home in Texas, to military jet intercept pilots, and even to Russian military divers chasing submerged UFOS (known as "USOs), and more.

Forbidden Planet. There would seem to be areas on our planet where we are "forbidden" to go for as long as anyone can remember. These are ancient areas. The local people of those regions named them accordingly. Some of these areas have been labeled for centuries with such blood chilling names that actually say flat out they are places of death, and labeled so as very clear warnings to all who consider venturing there.

Not Paranoia But A Real Occurrence? So the idea of UFOs being lethal, of there being a conspiracy to "get rid" of people who investigate them, and of suppressing information on a grand scale, even to the point of ruining careers and killings, is not so unlikely an idea at all, it seems. Furthermore, besides the "normal" abductions, cattle mutilations, and crop circles, the fact of disappearances of people, planes, and even villages, as well as ships and ship crews, is also a very disturbing thing. Oddly, even in many UFO books, these deadly encounters are barely mentioned.

Why not? Why hasn't the lethality of UFOs been related to us more, especially when often UFOs are sighted in and around the time that such fatal events occur. Yes, there are books on strange phenomena, but only rarely do they cross over and attempt to show a pattern of such events as being correlated to UFOs in any major or meaningful way. Nor do they attempt to really discuss the implications of such events.

Even then, such discussions are short in nature, as if they are almost a side matter to the main issue of the existence of UFOs. This, I think, is because most authors are still at the stage where they are attempting to prove the fact of the existence of UFOs, and so just haven't gotten around to dealing with the specifics of the injuries, deaths, and disappearances that seem so often to go along with them.

Nevertheless, what if they are not really a side issue? What if UFO deaths and injuries, cattle mutilations, and disappearances are the real issue? What if they form the primary one, and not just the "sightings" of alien spacecraft in our skies? What if UFOs are truly dangerous and that is the main issue? There does seem significant evidence to support this idea.

Something Is Going On. In this book, I intend to show a very real and bizarre thing is happening and has been happening for a long time. Something evil, something malevolent is going on. Whatever it is, it has dark and perilous implications for us all.

I intend to make a compelling case for just what is actually happening by listing cases, and then going on to explain possibly why this might be happening. I contend there is an ongoing suppression of the facts by "someone," possible reasons why this is so, and more frighteningly, what happens when some go so far as to refuse to give in, to "shut up," and continue to search for those reasons, despite being warned off, told not to do this.

With the conclusion of this chapter, let me ask you yet one more question; if the government is willing to resort to ultimate measures to maintain a lid of secrecy on the existence and/or reasons such things as UFOs appear in our skies, one has to ask why?

There are two main reasons why people commit coldblooded murders, and we're not talking about crimes of passion here, not killings done in the heat of the moment out of jealousy, hatred, or revenge. No, we're talking about deliberate, coldblooded, premeditated murders.

What are those reasons? The two primary ones are (1) because there is some great gain to be made by committing the murder (freedom, money, inheritance, power, maintenance of a secret, etc.), or (2) fear. People often commit murders out of fear.

So in conclusion of this chapter, ask yourself this; what is it the government wants so badly, it is willing to resort to repeated murders of innocents in order to get it? Or, and this may be far worse, what does the government fear so much that it will go to any lengths to stop people from learning more about whatever it is, the deep, dark secret?

As a correlation to this, also ask yourself the question: why are UFOs injuring and killing people? Why are they abducting them? Why are they mutilating cattle? If they are responsible, why are they making so many people, over so many years, simply disappear for good?

Is this because aliens might see as a reason worth it, to do such terrible things in order to win some great prize? Are they reaching for their version of some fabled "brass ring?" Alternatively, is it, too, out of fear? If so, what is it the aliens are so afraid of? Is it us? Something else? A combination of the two? Let's see what we can specifically deduce in the way of answers to these questions in the following chapters.

CHAPTER 4—JUST WHAT ARE UFOS?

"The brightest light casts the darkest shadow."
—Jess C. Scott, The Darker Side of Life

We won't dwell on this question long at all, since we all have a good idea of what UFOs are already. Our primary purpose here in Part One, the overview, in bringing it up at all, is simply to point out a few things that still may not be generally known, or perhaps even entirely unknown to some. In addition, it is to give the government's own and official definition of what constitutes a UFO. It is the one used throughout this book.

Caveat: First, as a caveat, it should be noted that despite many people being convinced UFOs do exist, many in positions of power and authority do not think this is true, or at least, they say this publicly. For instance, David Morrison, a member ("Fellow") of the Committee for Skeptical Inquiry argues there is little real evidence to support the contention UFOs even exist at all.

Many other skeptics feel the same way and loudly and stridently proclaim their contrary viewpoints in this regard to just about anyone who will listen. In their opinion, as with David Morrison, UFOs are, or should be, a non-issue, because they simply aren't real, and so therefore, are not a problem.

Yet, what if we reverse this logic of theirs? If not being real makes "something" a non-issue and not a problem as they say, then if something is an issue and a problem, well then, that should make that "something" real, right? If logic works in one direction, it should work then equally well in the other direction.

Since UFOs are, or have been a problem for many hundreds of thousands of people, perhaps millions of them, with regard to encounters, sightings, and abductions, then doesn't that automatically make UFOs real, so therefore an issue, and a major one at that by those skeptics' own logic? Of course, skeptics don't see it this way. For them, their logic only works in the one direction…just why this is so, and in defiance of all "logical" reasoning, is a question they seem unable and/or unwilling to answer. They simply shrug such ideas off with a blithe wave of their hand, as if the question is of no consequence.

Still, even if they admit nothing else, most of them will readily admit the subject has somehow, someway, seized control of, and captured the majority of the public's mind. The UFO topic has done so for many decades now.

UFOs, then, whatever one may believe with regard to their reality, have an amazingly persistent and consistent staying power in the public mind. It is an influence that has endured for more than half a century, at least, so far, and shows no sign of letting up.

Actually, statistics show that sightings and belief in UFOs are rising, not diminishing. So for those skeptics who said it was the anxiety of the Cold War with the old Soviet Union that caused people to think they saw such things, well the news is out: the Cold War, along with the Soviet Union, has been gone since the 1990's!

Yet, the sightings of UFOs are increasing, not diminishing. How can that be, if such a premise is correct? The answer is, of course, it can't be. Therefore, those skeptics were wrong. It wasn't a general anxiety or fear of a nuclear war that caused such UFO encounters and sightings. They were and are a real and separate phenomenon. They are not some anxiety, mass-induced delusion that has continued for over a century now, or even longer.

Moreover, this isn't just about the staying power of the UFO phenomenon we're talking about here. As mentioned, the number of annual sightings worldwide is climbing, not diminishing, so that the power and influence of UFOs on our society seems to be growing, not lessening.

No, the whole question of UFOs is not just a weird side effect of the Cold War of the 1950's, through the 1990's. Oddly, and despite all the predictions of the skeptics, sightings of UFOs didn't cease. Instead, as stated, sightings have grown, and continue to do so. The number of videos taken annually of such strange objects in the skies also grows on an annual basis, as more people acquire cellphones with camera capabilities.

The trend seems markedly against the skeptics in all these ways. In other words, the skeptics weren't just off the mark; they were categorically and uniformly wrong about their explanation for people "thinking" they were seeing strange objects in the skies. UFOs, it seems, were not a hysterical reaction by society to dark times at all. Rather, UFOs are a separate phenomenon in their own right.

Also, remember, these skeptics are pre-biased **not** to believe UFOs are real, and despite massive amounts of available evidence opposing this predisposed viewpoint of theirs. They approach the problem not just as skeptics, ones waiting to see enough evidence to prove something is true or untrue in an objective manner, but as being prone to not believing despite available evidence to the contrary. They have, even at the outset it seems, an almost vested interest, emotional or otherwise, in not believing in the existence of UFOs. This means skeptics are not objective in their viewpoints on the matter.

Why is there this predisposition to deny the existence of something on their part? How do we explain this? Well, this could be because they may simply not want to believe in the existence of UFOs, or at least would prefer not to. Perhaps, as mentioned earlier, the idea frightens them too much. Perhaps, they are too afraid of thinking humans might not be the top of the food chain. This would mean for skeptics that the idea they control their own destinies is a false one. Therefore, it might be understandable such people simply can't or don't want to conceive of extraterrestrials as being real.

This is a valid fear. Who would want to believe such a thing? Some just can't bring themselves to face such an idea. So perhaps some skeptics fall into this group of frightened people. Moreover, some UFO conspiracy theorists argue that some skeptics may have been cajoled into being so skeptical on purpose. They claim some may even have been paid in some way by "someone" to do this, refute the existence of all things extraterrestrial.

Whether or not this is the case, and I have no idea if it is or not, skeptics do seem to cling steadily to their skepticism, despite much evidence presented to them to the contrary on the actual existence of UFOs.

However, a few skeptics have actually come over to the believers' side, because in the process of their trying to debunk the idea, the evidence finally convinced a few of them UFOs are real.

Case In Point. The famous Dr. Josef Allen Hynek, who served on the original US Air Force Project Sign, as well as Project Grudge, and Project Bluebook, precisely because he was a scientist and such a skeptic of UFOs, was slowly converted to the idea there was enough empirical evidence to support the things actually existed. He's famous for a variety of reasons in this regard, and one of these is his development of the famous "Close Encounter System," which is now used to type and describe each type of possible encounter with a UFO. It also became part of the title of the movie, ***Close Encounters Of The Third Kind***.

Admittedly, the conversion of someone so famous to the idea UFOs exist is a rarity, but again, skeptics seem predisposed to disbelieve the idea, even before evidence is submitted to them. So even a few defections from their ranks is a notable thing. Even the very title of one organization, the "Committee for Skeptical Inquiry" shows the members are predisposed not to accept any available evidence, even of the most powerful nature and variety.

After all, it does make one wonder why they don't have the title of their group just be: "Committee for Inquiry," if their approach is an unbiased one, and their decisions solely based on the evidence supplied for or against. Adding the word, "Skeptical" says it all. They are, in other words, saying they "don't believe in UFOs," even before their inquiry starts. Therefore, it just might be they are actually being more cynical than skeptical. As Matthew Henry once said, *"there are none so blind as those who will not see."* This may be the case here.

However, if this is so, then they do have problems, because UFOs, no matter how one looks at them, skeptically or otherwise, are hardly a non-issue. People are seeing something. This alone should make the subject an issue, shouldn't it?

Because regardless of the cause, whether "real" or otherwise (mass hallucinations?), it is affecting the population of America and elsewhere around the world to an incredible degree.

There is a real social phenomenon going on here. If people are obsessing, swearing they see things that aren't there in ever-increasing numbers, and doing it in the millions already, surely this is grounds for some sort of ongoing research as to why this is so? Or are "mass hallucinations" just reaching epidemic proportions without a single "professional" caring about this happening at all?

That seems decidedly odd. The population of the world may be steadily going insane, if these are hallucinations and not a single group of professionals, whether doctors, astronomers, psychiatrists, or anyone else, cares to know or investigate why this is so? Again, very odd…

Besides this, many people of equal or far superior status to Mr. Morrison have seen UFOs, and this includes even presidents. President Jimmy Carter, for instance, saw one while Governor of Georgia. President Ronald Regan did, as well, before he became President. Other famous and political personages also have sighted such things. There are congressional representatives and senators who insist the phenomenon is real, based on their own personal experiences and/or evidence.

Mr. Morrison may be a skeptic, but powerful, influential, and celebrated officials of our government are not. For instance, Michael Gravel, a former senator, no less, insisted and still insists there is a deliberate attempt to suppress, discount, or ignore evidence concerning UFO sightings. He claims some in the White House are behind these efforts. This is from a U.S. Senator, no less! Are all these people liars or insane, including not only congressional representatives and senators, but presidents, as well? Such a thing would hardly seem likely.

The Fear Of Being Marginalized: Mr. Gravel is not alone. A number of high-ranking members of our military, various generals, astronauts, and other officers argue the same thing: that there is a deliberate effort to suppress evidence regarding UFOs.

They further claim those who are too insistent about this fact being true are subject to being deliberately "marginalized," as they put it in their own words. They also claim many eyewitnesses to UFOs in the military and elsewhere refuse to report the sightings for this reason, the extreme (and justified?) fear of being marginalized, or in other words, singled out as odd and therefore, untrustworthy to continue to do their jobs or to receive promotions otherwise due to them. In others words, reporting such things destroys careers.

So Just what constitutes a UFO sighting? What are those weird lights and objects we see in the sky? What are the criteria that make seeing something such an extraordinary event as to be a UFO?

Well, to keep this short and to the point, let's just go by the "official" definition. I think this is a reasonable basis or premise for judging as to what a UFO is, since it is the government's own.

In addition, this definition goes back to the beginning of modern sightings of UFOs. Air Intelligence at the Pentagon in 1947 received a requested report by the then Lieutenant General, Nathan Twining. At the time, he was in charge of the Air Materiel Command at Wright-Patterson, a military base and one many of us have certainly heard of with regard to UFOs.

The base has become infamous. It is synonymous with UFOs and aliens over the decades.

Lieutenant General Twining had sent a classified document to the then Brigadier General George Schulgen, who at the time was Chief of Air Intelligence. The main points stipulated in this now declassified memorandum as to what constituted valid UFO sightings were:

• **What is seen by a witnesses is determined to be real**, not the result of hallucinations, visions, or something of such a nature.

• **Most of the things seen (at the time of the report) were of a "disk" shape, of a good size, and did not appear to be natural, i.e., they appeared manmade or made by something or someone.** Since then, and even at the time and prior to then, other objects of different shapes have been seen, as well, such as "cigar-shaped" and more recently, "triangular-shaped" objects.

• **The things seen did not behave in any known or natural manner**, in that they had abilities no human aircraft had at the time, or even now, for that matter. These abilities include incredible maneuverability, the ability to dart almost haphazardly about the sky at impossible angles and speeds, and to do this very abruptly. They could attain extreme altitudes in mere seconds. Furthermore, due to the nature of these things responses to attempted interceptions, this lent credence to the idea they were being intelligently controlled and/or manipulated.

• **Descriptions of the UFOs included the fact the things reflected light, and so appeared often to be metallic in nature**. They also gave off light or had lights in many cases.

• **The UFOs seemed never to produce any sort of exhaust emissions, no "trails," or contrails visible to the

naked eye. It should also be noted here that many witnesses, the greatest number, report there is no discernible motor sound to the things they see, that more often than not, they are strangely silent. With rare exceptions, this seems to be so, although sometimes, sounds like distant hums or "buzzing" are reported.

• **The UFOs (again, at the time of the events and as reported by eyewitnesses then) were usually circular,** "disk-like" or perhaps "elliptical" in shape. Often, they appeared to be flat at the lower extremity (meaning the bottom—rather like a Frisbee in that regard) and to be rounded or "domed" on the upper extremity of the vehicle. In other words, many UFOs then and now seem to have the classic "flying saucer" shape to them.

• **Often, the UFOs are seen travelling in fleets or formations**. The number of individual UFOs in such a formation can vary, being anywhere from "three to nine" but sometimes more. However, since the time of this report, many witnesses have seen much larger formations that don't seem to be formations at all, but rather just large groupings or "flocks" of UFOs.

• **Speeds (at the time and even now), were often far in excess of the speed of sound, apparently, but with no accompanying sonic booms**. However, this didn't preclude the fact UFOs could also hover for long moments, before seemingly instantly attaining such incredible speeds. More recently, some UFOs have been clocked at truly remarkable speeds, able to traverse the diameter of the Earth in minutes at such velocities. In short, they seem to defy the laws of physics, as we now know them.

So there we have it, the "official" government description of what constitutes a UFO sighting.

Of course, with more sightings since then, the number and variety of shapes seen has steadily increased. Still, with only some minor adjustments to account for sightings since this report, we will use this same official definition here.

As a side note, if you should happen to see something like this, then you are probably seeing a genuine UFO. That is, you are, at least, according to the government's own officially requested definition of them. I would hope you would report such sightings to add to the growing body of evidence and knowledge about the subject.

Major Conclusion Of Official Report: One last thing about UFOs here before we move on; authorities state the report concluded the objects being witnessed were probably of "interplanetary," or extraterrestrial in origin, since nothing on Earth, either American or Soviet at the time, could perform in such an incredible manner, or have so many inconceivable capabilities.

In other words, the official report stated what UFOs looked like, how they behaved, and even where they probably came from, and that "where," as being way "out there" in space. In short, they were, and are not, of this world.

Well, now that we have the government's original definition of what constitutes UFO sightings and their probable origin as not being of this world; let's look at exactly what happens when more than just one witnesses an object or a light in the sky. Moreover, we'll discuss what happens when there are actual physical encounters, specifically, encounters that leave people injured, sick, or even dead. There are a lot more of these than you may think.

This completes Part 1, our overview on the subject of UFOs, and now I wish to focus on the actual harmful and deadly encounters many have had with these alien objects, as well as the ramifications and consequences of such specific cases.

PART 2—UFOS—THE KILLING FIELDS

"Behind the ostensible government sits enthroned an invisible government owing no allegiance and acknowledging no responsibility to the people."
—President Theodore Roosevelt

CHAPTER 5—DAMAGE CAUSED BY UFOS

"I've been convinced for a long time that the flying saucers are real and interplanetary. Another words we are being watched by beings from outer space."
—**Albert M. Chop, Deputy Public Relations Director, NASA**

Marshall County, Minnesota, August 1979. This is one of the better-documented UFO cases, because there is physical evidence in the form of damage to a vehicle. It all started in late summer for Sheriff Val Johnson. While on patrol in Marshall County, he spotted a strange light hovering, not far away from his vehicle. Since he was patrolling an area close to the Canadian border, his first suspicion was they might be smugglers trying to cross from Canada into the United States. This was not the case. At approximately 1:30 AM, Sheriff Johnson decided to investigate.

As he approached the strange light, he was amazed to find that instead of going away, it flew directly toward him at high speed. This is not what one would expect from smugglers trying to escape the law.

What followed is not clear for Sheriff Johnson. He remembers hearing the sound of glass shattering. Then, not quite an hour later, he heard the sound of the dispatcher trying to contact him over the patrol car's radio. This brought the sheriff to full consciousness.

He realized his car now blocked one of the lanes of the highway, being almost sideways to it. He told the dispatcher something had just hit his car, but he had no idea what. He had no recollection of anything at all in that regard, except for that last memory of the sound of breaking glass.

When help arrived, the situation was investigated. Sheriff Johnson realized his car had suffered considerable damage. The windshield was damaged. The antenna had been twisted. Lights had been broken and there was other damage, as well. As a further oddity, although the clock of the car still worked, as did Johnson's wristwatch, there were both 15 minutes behind the actual current time.

The only physical injury to the sheriff was his eyes felt painful. A doctor later said it was as if they had been exposed in too close a proximity to some type of "welding" equipment. Although, the doctor had no idea how this could have happened given the related circumstances. Neither did Sheriff Johnson, other than the light he remembered coming toward him might have caused the damage.

An investigation was conducted, not only by the police, but by Alan Hendrie for the Center for UFO Studies. Their joint conclusions were that a "high-velocity" object of some sort had passed directly over the patrol car. This had caused a pressure wave and so the resulting damage to the vehicle.

To this day, no explanation other than that of a big UFO has ever been proffered as to what happened to Sheriff

Johnson. Furthermore, the car is still available and can be seen with all the damage still there. Apparently, the local authorities chose not to repair it, because it was such an oddity.

Rosedale, Victoria, Australia, September 1980. This is another well-documented UFO encounter. Further, it's one resulting in injuries, as well as damage. Near the small town of Rosedale in Victoria, Australia, a ranch hand woke to the sound of his cattle being disturbed. Assuming this might be rustlers, he decided to investigate. However, instead of finding rustlers, the rancher was confronted by the site of a UFO. The upper portion of the craft was domed, but overall, the thing had a disk-like shape. Blue and orange lights flashed around the perimeter of the object.

What was even more frightening was how low the UFO was. It was barely 10 feet in the air. Then, it gained altitude. The UFO positioned itself over a water tank, one that could hold up to 10,000 gallons. Then, the ranch hand, using his motorcycle, raced towards the UFO. He described the thing as emitting a "whistling" sort of noise as he approached it.

At this point, accompanied by a screeching noise, a "black tube" came out of the bottom of the UFO and went into the tank. Then came a piercing noise. The ranch hand could only assume the thing was taking water on board through the tube. Then the object retracted the tube and flew off.

Where the vehicle had hovered so close to the ground, or perhaps even had landed on it, was a black ring of burned weeds. Within the circle was green grass, but and strangely enough, all the little yellow blossoms growing there had disappeared.

Upon inspecting the water tank, they found it was completely empty. The mud, which had collected over time at the bottom of the tank, was in a cone-like shape. This, for the ranch hand, was clear evidence the water had been sucked out, as if by the process of some sort of vacuum, rather than having been drained out by means that were more conventional.

The event was not over, at least not for the ranch hand. He became ill, and suffered from headaches. Moreover, he also had nausea. The symptoms continued for over a week. The cause of the illness was never determined, but that it was associated with the UFO seems likely.

As a side note, that December, a small reservoir not far from there, near Bundalaguah, had its water drained as well. Moreover, a mysterious black ring was discovered in the grasses nearby, which looked the same as the one discovered at the ranch. Was the UFO using the local water supplies for its own purposes? It seems likely.

Again, there are more cases of such types of damage, but these are not the primary concern here. Rather, they are meant only to illustrate that damage does occur with UFO encounters in some, if not many cases. These being such well-documented ones, they serve as good examples of the types of damages UFOs can cause.

CHAPTER 6—INJURIES

"We are all like the bright moon, We still have our darker side."
—Gibran Khalil Gibran

Because of limited space here in this book, as well as for reasons of using only those cases that have the best verification, I wish to keep the mentioned UFO injuries to only those that are the best documented, and I don't even have room here for all of those, or this book would simply be far too lengthy.

However, the ones chosen should certainly suffice to prove our point in this chapter. Moreover, one cannot underestimate the severity of some interactions with UFOs.

For instance, UFO investigator, Jerome Clark, made a startling statement in his article *Why UFOs Are Hostile*. He stresses the point that interacting with UFOs can be a very dangerous business, indeed. He points out that according to a variety of reports; verified ones, that people have been assaulted, burned, and often made to suffer illness from radiation.

Moreover, he adds that UFOs have chased people in their vehicles. They have attacked their homes. They have caused major power failures and in some cases, these power disruptions affect our military bases, as well as nuclear missile facilities. Mr. Clark goes on to say there even have been on-the-spot cremations of some individuals.

There is something more that Mr. Clark and I agree upon. He feels that other than contactees saying the occupants of UFOs are friendly, there seems to be no evidence for this. Again, Jerome Clark and I are in complete accordance on this point.

In any case, here are some of the more well-known and documented examples of injuries caused by UFOs.

I am not listing these in order of their importance, but rather by date, to give the reader a sense of the timeline of modern UFO sightings with regard to injuries:

Injuries, Brazil, 1957. A wave of UFO sightings and encounters occurred in this country, ones that resulted in witnesses not only being injured in the ordinary sense one might expect, but for a number of them, the suffering of strange "burns," as well. These burns were not all from one UFO sighting, but received by different people over a number of different sightings, which are commonly referred to as "waves."

Injuries, Itapúa, Brazil, at a military base there, two guards witnessed a bright orange saucer in the sky. This was around two in the morning on November 4, and so completely dark at the time. The saucer-like object, which had been moving across the sky, then paused over the two guards, as if knowing they were there, as one of them later put it.

The guards felt immense heat, as if they had been set afire. In agony, they shrieked aloud. This alerted other soldiers who responded. Some of these managed to see the UFO before it shot off into the night sky, even as the fort's electricity ceased to function at the same time.

Such electrical disturbances, as many UFO buffs know, often seem to accompany sightings of such craft, as if their mere presence causes electromagnetic disruptions. The two soldiers were then taken to emergency care at a military-controlled hospital, where it was determined they had suffered burns to at least ten percent of their bodies. Although not overtly life threatening, they were still serious.

Injuries, Orogrande, New Mexico. As coincidental as it may seem, later on that same day, November 4, several people had their vehicles suddenly cease to function on a New Mexican highway. This was on a lonely stretch of paved road at a time when the population of New Mexico was very small. Witnesses described an ovoid, an egg-shaped UFO appearing above them and coming closer to where the people were stranded along with their vehicles.

This, they probably rightly assumed, was the cause of the engine failures of their cars somehow, since it was just too strange to be a mere coincidence. One person, the closest to the UFO, later showed a bad case of what was described as "sunburn" at the time, although he'd only been standing outside of his vehicle for just a few minutes.

Others, standing further from the UFO, suffered no such injuries. An important thing to note here is that "sunburn" is actually a form of radiation burn, if normally a very mild one, although in some cases severe. Furthermore, too much exposure resulting from repeated sunburns has been strongly linked to skin cancers.

Injuries, Merom, Indiana. Two days later, on November 6, a UFO appeared over a farm near the small town of Merom. The farmer, René Gilham, stated the thing emitted an intense bright light, which illuminated the immediate area to an incredible degree. He, too, suffered burns to his face as a proximate cause of this "light." These burns were bad enough to result in his hospitalization for two days in order to receive intensive treatment. There was no doubt in the mind of the attending physician the burns were somehow radiation induced, although he had no idea as to what type of radiation it might be that had caused them.

Injuries, Madison, Ohio. November 10, at approximately 1:30 in the morning, a UFO hovered behind a woman's house. She claimed to have observed it for about thirty minutes and described the object as being "acorn-shaped." This description was to be repeated again several times in other incidents in later years, including the now infamous Kecksburg Incident in Pennsylvania.

Over the next few days, she suffered from increasing vision problems, as well as having a strange rash spread over her body. Upon seeing her doctor, she was informed her symptoms were akin to those of radiation exposure, but just what type of radiation it was, again, is unknown.

Just what was going on during this year, this "wave" of UFO sightings starting in Brazil and then working their way northward and east across the United States is a matter of conjecture. However, whatever the reason or cause, the results were remarkably the same for eyewitnesses who were too close to the UFOs. Radiation sickness and poisoning, as well as burns were reported over a wide area of the western hemisphere.

These burns, hair falling out, rashes, eye damage, etc., seem to be the hallmark of many symptoms of witnesses of UFOs of the time. However, this sort of thing didn't end that year, but continued. The same symptoms were reported repeatedly over the following decades and more often than one might believe reasonably possible.

Valensole, France, 1965. Maurice Masse, a farmer was just preparing to start his day's work. This was when he saw an aircraft approach and land in one of his fields. He went to investigate. He saw an oval object supported by four landing "legs." Two beings were also there, standing just in front of the aircraft. Short, no more than four feet in height, they wore greenish-gray uniforms. They had large heads, sharp-pointed chins, and almond-shaped eyes. He describes them as emitting a sort of grumbling sound, but whether this was language or not, he couldn't tell. Whatever it was, it had no meaning for him.

As he approached, one of the beings raised an arm. He held what Masse described as a "pencil-like" object in it. The creature pointed it at him. Instantly, Masse felt paralyzed. He couldn't move at all. As he stood there, the creatures entered their egg-shaped craft and departed. Masse, unfortunately, was still paralyzed and he would remain so for approximately another twenty minutes. If he had needed to move even to save his life, he couldn't have.

There was actual evidence of this encounter, and therefore, it is one of the earlier and better cases for this reason. There was a hole or depression and a damp region around it where the UFO had landed. This wet earth soon became very hard. Furthermore, vegetation in the immediate area died. In addition, investigation of the soil in and around the hole showed a much higher than normal amount of calcium compared to samples taken farther away from the site. Although Masse eventually recovered from the paralysis, he felt it had been a terrifying experience.

Winnipeg, Manitoba, Canada, 1967. In May, while exploring an area around Falcon Lake for minerals, Stephen Michalak witnessed two UFOs, oval in shape. One of them landed not far from where he stood. With caution, he approached the objects, curious as to what they might be.

He claimed to have heard a strange, steady, low noise. There was also a strong smell of sulfur (rotten egg odor). On the lower hemisphere was what appeared to be some type of hatch or door. Michalak claimed he could hear voices issuing from within. These seemed human enough in sound, if of a higher pitch. Michalak said he could hear two such voices.

Assuming the craft might have been some new type of government military vessel, he called out. There was no response from within. He peered through the open hatchway, but all he could make out was a dazzling array of lights, or as he described them, *"a maze of lights."* Abruptly, the hatchway closed, panels sliding into place across it and blocking any view of the interior of the vessel. Michalak touched the hull of the craft. This was so hot; he was burned, despite wearing gloves at the time.

The craft shot upward, even as stumbled backwards. As he described it, hot air vented down toward the ground. So intense was the heat, Michalak's shirt ignited. At the same time, he felt extremely nauseous.

Fearing for his health, Michalak arrived shortly later at a hospital. He had burns on his chest. They were in the same shape and style as the grid the hot air from the ship had blasted at him. His health worsened. Later, he had to go to the Mayo Clinic in Minnesota as a result.

Moreover, despite official investigations, as well as civil ones, nothing more could be found out about the incident, or so the government said. Yet, many felt the government was deliberately covering up something, since no explanation at all seemed forthcoming.

Much later, years in fact, in 1975, some members of Parliament demanded the government release findings they felt sure they had in their possession. Nothing was ever released in this regard, with the Canadian government denying it had any such materials, which on the face of it seems very strange, indeed. Was there no investigation at all, despite a Canadian citizen having been made so ill by something and someone unknown?

Fargo/Bismarck, August 1975. Sandy Larson, her teenage daughter, and her daughter's boyfriend were on their way from Fargo, North Dakota to Bismarck. Not long after leaving Fargo, while traveling I-94, they saw something. To the south, was a brilliant flash, followed by a reverberating sound. Sandy described it as a "rumble." Then, flying swiftly towards the east, they saw ten objects. The craft seemed to have, as Sandy again put it, "smoke" engulfing them. Nine of the objects were approximately the same size, but one was much larger, or so it looked to the witnesses.

The UFOs came closer. Then, they abruptly descended, just yards from where the stunned passengers sat in their vehicle, staring at them. Suddenly, five of the things took off, disappearing. At this point, the witnesses describe undergoing a short period of paralysis, as if they had been "stuck" for several seconds. After this, the objects rose and sped off, disappearing over the horizon.

It took a moment for the three to realize they were now sitting in different positions within the vehicle. Sandy sat in the front seat, along with her daughter's boyfriend. However, Jackie, Sandy's daughter, who had been sitting between them in the front, now sat on her own in the back seat. As with many such cases, the three people had experienced some "missing time." Now time had passed for which they could not account.

This preyed on their minds. Finally, concerned, but sometime later, Sandy decided she and her daughter should go to the University of Wyoming, where a psychologist would place them under hypnosis and probe the missing time segment of their lives. Jackie's boyfriend, however, refused to be involved in this procedure, and so did not join them on their trip.

Under hypnosis, Jackie remembered being in a state of paralysis. Sandy claimed she had been made to float into the alien spacecraft. Here, some sort of medical-like examination was performed on her. This included a probe inserted inside of her nose (many abductees say this happens to them). She remembered feeling extremely nauseous during this and other procedures. After this, she and the others were returned to their car. All memory of the incident subsequently vanished.

This seems to have ended the incident. Although Sandy and her daughter, Jackie, believe the event as described under hypnosis took place, I have no other corroborating evidence, other than the countless tales of other abductees in such situations and the extreme similarity of all of them.

Injuries, Brazil, 1976. In Quixada, a man by the name of Luis Barroso Fernandez was going about his business of herding his livestock. This was on April 3, of 1976. He had just finished his task and was returning to his ranch when he noticed a humming noise, one louder than any insects would naturally make. He said the noise was similar to something akin to the sound huge bees might make.

He paused in his journey to ascertain the source of the noise. Finding no particular cause for the phenomenon, he finally continued down the trail with his donkey. Then, out of nowhere it seemed, a brilliant sphere of light (he later said it was approximately some three meters in diameter), passed right above him.

The light then descended and Luis realized it was an aircraft of some unknown sort, but one round in shape. His donkey panicked and bolted at the same moment a ray of brilliant illumination engulfed them both. Luis says the light paralyzed both him and his animal.

Then, an opening appeared in the craft. Two beings came out, one with a tubular device, which it pointed at Luis. The light from the device struck him full in the face and he then promptly passed out.

About two hours later, Luis regained consciousness. He said his face felt hot, flushed, as if he'd somehow been burned. His breathing felt labored. He suffered from a massive headache.

Luis Barroso did not get better. In fact, his condition steadily worsened. His hair whitened, literally "overnight," as witnesses reportedly described it. He had trouble with his mind, struggled to remember things in the days and weeks that followed. He fought to be able to concentrate. Luis' mental capabilities steadily diminished in this way over time, until he wasn't even capable of taking care of himself. It is reported he ended up with the equivalent intellectual capacity of a mere toddler.

Ultimately, about fifteen years later, he died, having been declining in his health throughout all this time. In short, Luis was ultimately a fatal victim of his UFO incident. His encounter first sickened him, destroyed his mind, his livelihood, and then his independence. Ultimately, his encounter seems to have resulted in his death. However, since this occurred so long after the original sighting, I place it here in the "injured" category for this reason. In any case, the cause of his illnesses was never ascertained by the doctors.

Injuries, Piney Woods, Huffman, Texas, 1980, "A Diamond On Fire." This sighting is considered a classic by most ufologists, because it is so well documented, complete with doctors' reports and photographs of the victims' symptoms and illnesses. You may have seen its reenactment on any of several different television shows about UFO events in recent years, just because it is such a famous incident. Nevertheless, it does materially advance our case that UFOs cause injuries and more, so I felt it had to be included here, as well.

The date was December 29, 1980. Two women, Betty Case, aged 51 at the time, and Vickie Lundrum, aged 57, were traveling a secluded stretch of rural highway, which passed through an area known as Piney Woods. Along for the ride was Colby, the grandson of Vickie. He was just seven years old at the time of the event.

After driving in this isolated region for a while, they spotted a light shining ahead of them. It moved slowly, just above treetop level. At first, they paid little attention, assuming it was just an aircraft of some sort passing overhead, possibly a helicopter, judging by its slow rate of progress. However, as it approached them, the light took on a distinct shape, that of a diamond. They then realized they were viewing an unfamiliar object.

Of course, they were confused. The area was very rural, consisting of woods combined with ponds and wetland. Being so isolated, and unpopulated an area, this limited possible causes for the light. So if not a helicopter or plane, just what were they viewing?

Moments later, the thing was directly ahead and floating just above them over the road. As they described it, frequent jets of what looked like red flames shot down from the craft splashing on to the road.

"*A diamond on fire,*" is the way Vickie described it. So overwhelmed was she, she became convinced this was a sign the world was ending, the Rapture was finally occurring, since as a Born Again Christian, her beliefs colored her perception of things, and so her resulting interpretation of the event. Unlike with so many other UFO cases, this object made a noise, a steady "bleeping."

Betty halted their vehicle, afraid to approach closer to the object. She noticed the interior of the car was now uncomfortably hot, so everyone climbed out of the vehicle. They stood there on the road. They just stared at the diamond-shaped object as it continued its strange, fiery display in the night darkness. The UFO emitted a new and continuous loud noise now, a sort of "roar."

In fear for the safety of the boy, Colby, his grandmother returned him to the car. She then sat with him to keep him safe. Betty remained outside the vehicle, alone now. She continued to watch the UFO.

Then, helicopters appeared. To quote Betty, "*They seemed to rush in from all directions.*" The helicopters appeared military in nature and she felt they were probably from one of several military installations nearby.

The UFO began to ascend, whereupon it took off in a southwesterly direction. The helicopters now followed and seemed to be chasing the strange object. Assuming the event was now over as she watched them fly off into the night, Betty started to enter her vehicle, only to find the door handle burned her, so heated had it become. The interior of the car was stifling. As swiftly as they could, they all headed home.

As they traveled a section of freeway, they could see the UFO off in the distance, with the helicopters surrounding it, as if in an attempt to corral the thing, perhaps even force it to land. At this point, they confidently identified 23 helicopters, including several CH047 Chinook copters. However, not all were of this type, but just some.

Later, upon having reached home, the two women and Colby began to feel ill. Over several hours, their conditions worsened. Betty's symptoms were inflamed with swollen eyes, along with blisters on her neck and head. Nausea accompanied these symptoms.

Still, they did not yet seek medical help. However, by the following morning, Betty was very ill, barely conscious. Both Vickie and Colby suffered, as well, but not to such an extreme extent. Vickie, less affected, nursed Betty.

Why they didn't' seek immediate medical attention at this point is uncertain, other than the long journey involved to do so, the high costs of emergency treatment, and a general reluctance, perhaps, just to go to the hospital. Ultimately, they decided this was best, despite their hesitations in the matter, and so they went. Colby and Vickie also felt the need for some medical aid, as well, although again, their symptoms, though definite ones, were not as extreme as Betty's appeared.

Betty underwent care normally associated with burn patients. The odd thing was that unlike normal burn victims, her hair began falling out, which seemed more a symptom of radiation poisoning to the doctors than the result of more "normal" burns.

As her treatment continued, Colby, too, had problems with swelling and inflammation around his eyes. Vickie also was beginning to experience hair loss. At this point, all of them were receiving treatment as if they'd been exposed to radiation. It was all the doctors could think to do. Other symptoms, over time, included serious loss of weight, skin lesions, as well as skin cancers. Again, these are all symptoms of radiation sickness.

When attempts were made to follow up on the incident, they led nowhere. All the local military claimed no knowledge of the event, or admitted to any of their helicopters being involved. Major Tony Geishauser publicly stated that none of his helicopters from Fort Hood was involved, at least not to his knowledge.

However, there were some physical signs the event, in fact, had occurred, and this is besides the symptoms of the three witnesses. The asphalt where they claimed the sighting took place had suffered some type of damage that then required road repairs. The repairs, which normally might have taken months or more to be scheduled, let alone actually completed, were accomplished incredibly swiftly, as if someone had been pressured to remove the evidence just as quickly as possible.

A number of other witnesses saw the strange light, as well as sighting helicopters. A police officer and his wife, while driving, saw the UFO, as well as seeing some Chinook helicopters. This, despite the military insisting no helicopters had been sent. Another witness reported seeing a fleet of helicopters, as well, and he claimed to have seen them flying directly above him, very close, so there could be no mistake as to what they were. Yet another person, an oil worker, saw the UFO.

Finally, in a weird side note, in the spring of 1981, Vickie, along with a friend, and Colby, paid a visit to a Chinook helicopter on display at a show. According to both the friends' testimony, as well as Vickie's, the pilot said he had been flying the night of the incident, and had been ordered to respond to a UFO sighting. Again, this is despite a full denial of the military that any copters had been in the air at the time or in that region.

However, upon learning of the witnesses' illnesses and involvement, the pilot's attitude abruptly changed. He refused to speak further on the subject, hurriedly ushered them off the craft, and later denied any involvement with UFOs. Despite this, the testimony of Vickie and her friend still stands.

Therefore, there certainly seems sufficient corroboration to the testimonies of Betty, Vickie, and Colby, as well as that of their friend. Combined with their well-documented symptoms, the sightings by others, the pilot of the Chinook, and the damage to the road, this then forms a UFO sighting with considerable evidence to support the contention the event really took place.

Meanwhile, it seems strongly to indicate the government/military had lied about involvement in the whole affair. In other words, there had been a cover up. The official outcome of the investigation into the incident was the three had apparently witnessed some unknown aircraft, one whose origins were also unknown. In addition, the report stated they had been exposed to some type of radiation, in all probability an ionizing type. This leaves open the question of just which specific type of radiation it was, since many forms of radiation fit the category.

So upset were Betty, Vicki, and their grandson, Colby, by all this apparent subterfuge on the part of the government, they filed a lawsuit against the federal government in an attempt to recover the costs of their expensive medical treatment. However, while at a congressional hearing, the Inspector General for the army claimed no government interference in the events, and held the government was not liable for any such injuries. This, despite much evidence to the contrary and the testimony of other witnesses.

There Are More. I could go on at some considerable length here with regard to injuries by UFOs, because there are many more such types of incidents. For example, In Brazil, in 1977 there were a whole series of events where people claimed to have been "hunted" and "chased" by UFOs that struck them with beams (various colors), and who felt they had been targeted and chased by the UFOs, as if they were *"deliberately being hunted,"* as one witness put it.

The most common form of visible effects from this "hunting" was "burns and puncture wounds." The illnesses later often involved anemia of one sort or another, as well, and a general feeling of malaise, or weakness. So prevalent were these reports, so often were there attacks, and so widespread were they, the Brazilian government sent investigators to the Colares area. This was partly just in order to stem a growing tide of panic spreading around the region there.

This investigation was known as *Operação Prato*, in Portuguese (the main language of Brazil), or in English, "Operation Saucer." However, before any results were announced, the Brazilian government removed all the researchers and then promptly declared any information they'd obtained classified.

In short, as one person remarked, *"they just clammed up."* The situation remained this way until the 1990s. The nickname for the UFOs doing the attacks was *"chupas-chupas."*

The odd thing about this affair was the huge number of UFOs reported, along with the fact they varied so in sizes and shapes. Moreover, the widespread fear resulting from these attacks should not be underestimated. Many women, along with their children, evacuated the area completely. They left the men behind to protect their things while they sought safer places to stay. One can only imagine the economic disruptions, as well as the personal disruptions to all these people's lives.

In addition, the injuries again sound markedly like those of radiation sickness. As one doctor, Doctor Wellaide Cecim Carvalho, reported:

"All of them had suffered lesions to the face or the thoracic area." The *lesions, looking like radiation injuries, [they] "began with intense reddening of the skin in the affected area. Later the hair would fall out and the skin would turn black. There was no pain, only a slight warmth. One also noticed small puncture marks in the skin. The victims were men and women of varying ages, without any pattern."*

Again, we have those burn marks as we have had in other cases mentioned, as well as "lesions," hair falling out, skin disorders, etc. This seems very consistent with reports of other injuries by UFO encounters in other times and places over the decades where "ionizing radiation" was the probable cause of the injuries.

Furthermore, the noted billionaire, Robert Bigelow, a person deeply involved in the UFO phenomenon, in a New York Times article stated that:

"People have been killed. People have been hurt. It's more than observational kind of data."

The telling point in this comment is where Mr. Bigelow says that it's "more than observational data." Really? What other sources besides "observational" did Mr. Bigelow have available to him, ones we as the public, don't seem to have access to? Does having money, in this instance really give him a better access to information than just the usual sources available to the public? Was he privy to knowledge most of the rest of us are not? The old saying, "money talks" may be truer than most people realize, if so. If it doesn't "talk," it at least, seems to help "inform."

One very important point; I have only spoken of direct physical injuries to people from UFO encounters here, the kind reported by medical professionals, witnesses, and even ones that were photographed (the injuries), as with the Cash/Landrum case. These are verifiable, matter-of-record injuries, and there are more, many more such examples of this type.

However, I don't feel repeating a long, (bordering on endless) litany of more cases with more injuries will make our case stronger for the idea of UFOs causing humans physical harm. Either one accepts these documented cases, or one doesn't. They are easy enough to check, being such prominent ones. There are many independent and verifiable sources for them. Some of these are included in the references section at the end of this book.

Something else we should remember, as well; I haven't even discussed the idea of alien abductions here. Yet, estimates are there could be several "*million*" of these events, as well. Certainly, if so, they constitute injuries of a form, since the victims were kidnapped, taken without their agreement and against their will, and then often subjected to painful procedures, which in many cases, left scars, literally.

These, in my opinion, constitute injuries from UFO encounters, as well. However, without actual verifiable photographs and only testimony to go by, I decided not to include them here in our injuries catalog of UFO events. This doesn't mean I don't think they actually happened.

On the contrary, I do. I am certain that in many cases, such abductions really took place. However, for the purposes of this book, again, I wish to rely on more heavily documented accounts with substantial and different types of evidence to support them, and not just the testimony of witnesses, often while having undergone hypnosis, alone, to obtain such testimony.

Moreover, something else I haven't included here is the psychological repercussions to individuals, the damage to their psyches from enduring such events and illnesses. However, these are a very real form of injury, as well. People, such as the Lundrums, suffered intense psychological injury and over long periods. They also suffered economic hardships.

Animal mutilations are also another form of injury suffered by victims of UFO incidents, and although not injuries to humans, such animal and livestock deaths do have to be considered in all this, too. Animals are first horribly maimed and then killed in their thousands. If humans did this, they would be up on charges of felony cruelty to animals.

These mutilations seem to be caused by UFOs, are too often and too closely associated with sightings of them to think otherwise. Since some of these are well documented, including with photographs and autopsy reports, I will include a few you may not have heard of later on in this book.

CONCLUSION: The idea that the witnessing of and/or encountering UFOs ending by causing real physical harm to people, sometimes of truly major proportions, is not a new one, but it does seem to have been one played down by many researchers of UFOs in their books. Oh, they cite such cases, but then don't seem to go any further, draw any conclusions from this.

I can only assume the reason for this lack of focus or in-depth analysis of this aspect of the UFO phenomenon by such researchers is not because they aren't aware of this. Certainly, they are. Rather, it is more likely a result of them being so focused on the overall phenomenon, that a "few injuries" as many probably see it, although of importance, shouldn't be their primary concern. For such investigators, the goal seems to be to use the reports of injuries as added proof that UFOs exist.

My feeling is the opposite. This injury aspect of the UFO phenomenon is very disturbing. I feel it should be of primary concern, therefore. If people are being repeatedly injured by encounters with extraterrestrial flying vehicles and/or alien meetings, then this should be important.

Such injuries should signify there is a strong element of danger for humans in such encounters. Therefore, rather than injuries proving UFOs exist, acting as evidence for them, I feel that UFOs do exist (there being ample other forms of evidence for this fact already), and the injuries prove UFOs can be very dangerous to us. This is my crucial point here; UFOs can be dangerous to us. They can inflict major injuries to those victims who happen to be involved in such encounters.

The question then becomes: "Why?" If the aliens are our friends, are "our space brothers," ones only here to help and guide us along the path of our evolution as a species, then why these injuries? Some of these are quite deliberate in nature, even life threatening. Moreover, even if not deliberately caused injuries, they sometimes result from the extraterrestrials simply not seeming to care, or to put it bluntly, just not giving a damn about our safety one way or the other. They don't seem to use any caution as to how close they get to their human victims with their craft. They sometimes actively seem to seek us out, and thus endanger those people with radiation poisoning, etc.

No. There is more to this than just the occasional mere chance accident. For whatever reasons, UFOs have endangered people in our skies and on the ground. If their primary concern was to help, guide, and protect us, why do this? The answer, of course, is they wouldn't. That's our point in this chapter. Extraterrestrials from another world would not seek us out, even hunt us down at times, and harm us in such ways, if they were truly a benevolent species with only kind intentions towards us. It seems they are not.

CHAPTER 7—UFOS KILLING PEOPLE?

"The individual is handicapped by coming face to face with a conspiracy so monstrous he cannot believe it exists."
—J. Edgar Hoover, First Director, F.B.I.

In the last chapter, we've discussed physical injuries to some humans when they experienced close encounters with UFOs. Now, I think it is imperative to point out that in many of the cases; the humans did not actively seek out these encounters. They often did not approach the object at all when they saw one. If they did, they didn't move too closely to such bizarre craft, but often kept what they felt was a safe distance, as with the Lundrums in the Piney Woods Incident.

Understandably, many people were simply too frightened to approach such objects too closely. This is especially since these encounters often took place in isolated locations in the middle of the night, and there was no help readily available nearby should they get into trouble. Then, in addition, there is the strong fear of the unknown. Although undoubtedly curious, most people would simply be too fearful to get too near a strange, alien-looking spacecraft.

That is, unless they somehow felt reassured it was safe enough to do so. Most people (although, not all), choose to stand at a safe distance (as they determined it) and to observe the encounter from afar, instead. However, the question then is; what is a safe distance? It turns out it isn't always the same.

What exactly is our point here? Most of these people didn't just walk up to UFOs and so thereby took the responsibility upon themselves for suffering injuries they otherwise wouldn't have received, if they hadn't gotten so close. Instead, in many cases, the UFOs seemed to *seek them out*. They come to them whether the people wanted them to or not. Nobody asked a UFO to hover in front of them on a dark road, or hover just feet above their garage for the better part of half an hour, or land on their farms, etc.

Yes, admittedly, there are those who approached closely to UFOs on the ground, or when hovering close to it, but this was only after they felt it was reasonably safe to do so, or their innate curiosity just overwhelmed their common sense.

However, most encounters don't involve people going right up to and touching an alien spacecraft, with some exceptions, of course. Still, for the most part, it does seem to be the other way around. Alien craft seem to "take notice" of someone's presence and then proceed to interact with them in some manner.

People have been followed on highways, had UFOs zoom ahead and block their progress down a road. They have hovered close by over their homes, over their farms, and ranches. One has to ask; for what reason? Why do this?

Surely, whoever operates these craft, being supposedly intelligent, must be aware they can cause harm, injuries, and illness to anyone who gets too close to them, even if only as a side effect? If not in the beginning with their interactions with us humans, then over time, certainly even the dullest alien individuals should have been able to figure such a thing out, have learned there were inherent dangers for innocent bystanders who came too near them?

If that's the case, then the injuries should have slowed to a mere trickle over time, or even stopped altogether. This hasn't happened. Besides, I am talking decades of this sort of thing happening, and perhaps even centuries, or millennia. Therefore, it's hard to believe intelligent beings from another world wouldn't be aware of the harm their craft might inflict on humans over such durations of time. Either they had to be incredibly stupid not learn this at some point, or "they" just don't care. That's a major worry for us all, if so.

Furthermore, going beyond just seeking people out, there are those numerous cases in various locations around the world, including Colares, Brazil, where the victims claimed the UFOs actively *chased and hunted them down*, and struck them with "beams" or rays of light, as if engaging in target practice of some sort. This is hardly the fault of the victims being incautious in such a case, of approaching the extraterrestrial craft too closely, not when they are being chased through the jungles to avoid them! Furthermore, we're not just talking about a handful of people here, but many.

Putting aside what happens in the way of physical and psychological damage to people who claim to be abducted, the numerous deaths of animals, the strange animal mutilations occurring in such huge numbers worldwide, even putting all this aside, there are still the matter of human deaths. There are more of these than you might think.

Most of us may be aware of the fact there have been "one or two deaths" resulting from encounters with UFOs and so tend to chalk these up to just being "accidental," just as they have with injuries. However, there have been far more fatalities than just a couple of them.

Now, we'll discuss some examples of these deaths, the best-documented ones, but with one strange exception, which I wanted to include here first just because it is so very odd:

The *Ourang Medan* Death Ship Mystery, February1948 (Alternative Date: June 1947). Ships traveling in or near the Malacca Straits, a narrow body of water located between Malaysia and Sumatra picked up what they claim were SOS signals of a vessel in need of help. At the time, just what vessel was sending them was a mystery. However, the contents of the SOS were clear enough:

"*All officers including captain are dead, lying in chartroom and bridge. Possibly, whole crew dead.*" This communication was followed by a burst of indecipherable Morse Code, then a final, grim message: '*I die.*'"

Thanks to the signal having been received by not only two American vessels, but two others, as well, a source position for the transmission was determined. This also gave the likely vessel sending the message, the *Ourang Medan*.

The vessel, the *Silver Star* was sent to answer the distress summons. In mere hours, the *Silver Star* managed to intercept the *Quarang Medan*. There was no sign of movement about the decks or superstructure of the ship, no signs of human activity at all. Furthermore, all efforts to hail the distressed vessel brought no response. A boarding party went to investigate.

They found bodies. All had facial expressions of horror on them, eyes wide, mouths stretched open. There was even a dog that died while baring its teeth at something no longer there. Some bodies had an arm "pointing upwards" toward the sky. All the other bodies were on their backs, and their sightless eyes still stared heavenwards.

They found still more bodies below in various places, including in the boiler section. The perplexing thing was all seemed to have died in the same way. There was no sign of any of the crewmembers (or the dog) having been physically assaulted or injured in any way. Although later theories involved the possibility of methane gas from the sea, some illegal cargo of nerve gas, or even carbon monoxide poisoning, none of these were consistent with the way the bodies were found, the expressions on their faces, etc.

The last part of this story was the demise of the ship. The would-be rescuers noticed smoke coming from below. They had intended to tow the vessel, but for safety reasons, had to let it go. There was a massive explosion and the *Quarang Medan* sank shortly after they managed this. One description states the explosion was so massive; the ship seemed actually to lift out of the water for a moment.

A weird addition to this story is later, when various people tried to investigate the incident through the usual resources available for such purposes, they couldn't find the ship had ever even existed. That is, at first. Subsequently and only much later, evidence surfaced in Germany of the ship's actual existence, its name, and other information about it.

However, it seems as if all paperwork regarding the vessel had somehow either just disappeared or been mysteriously removed on purpose from the standard places such material normally would have been stored. Lloyds of London, being just one example of such a place that held no reference to the *Quarang Medan,* but definitely should have.

That the ship did exist is now not really in doubt. It did. How or why it vanished is a subject of conjecture, controversy, and a host of theories. Because of the way in which the bodies were found, the expressions of horror, the arms of several victims pointing toward the sky, the snarling dog, and the complete lack of any other signs of cause of death, many believe the ship encountered a hostile UFO and/or aliens.

As to what really happened to the *Quarang Medan*, only the dead, and perhaps a few unknown others, know. One thing is certain; no survivors or former crew of the *Quarang Medan* have ever come forward. No one has ever been heard to tell any sort of tales of their time aboard ship or its untimely destruction.

Since sailors are known for this sort of thing, the "spinning of yarns," and "tall tales," this in itself is very bizarre. Sometime over the succeeding decades, some of them, somewhere, should have mentioned something if any had survived. The only conclusion one can reasonably reach is there probably weren't any survivors of that ship. This lends further credence to the story being authentic. Since proof of the ship is there, but there are no crewmembers who ever even once mentioned anything ever about it, something must have happened to prevent them from doing so. That "something" was most likely their death onboard the vessel.

The whole incident remains one of the stranger mysteries, not least because it appears there were determined attempts to wipe out knowledge of the ship having ever existed. If this is so, it didn't work, but only because those who might have perpetrated such an attempt failed to find all the possible sources where the ship had been mentioned or listed.

Author and astronomer, Morris Jessup, proposed the theory the crew of the *Ourang Medan* might have been the victims of a UFO attack or encounter. Mr. Jessup referred to this in his, *The Case For The UFO* book.

The alternative theory, that there might have been some deadly gas aboard, doesn't seem to be supported due to a lack of evidence of symptoms, but instead, other unusual symptoms displayed by the dead. No known type of nerve gas would have left the bodies in such a way, with such contorted expressions of horror, for instance. Neither do such gases account for some of the dead pointing toward the sky, as if struck down while doing so.

For these reasons, I felt the story of the ill-fated *SS Ourang Medan* should be included here, although I freely admit, it is not the best-documented case in some regards. Still, since so few seem to have heard of this event, and the circumstances were so very bizarre to say the very least, and there does seem to have been a definite cover-up with regard to the ship even having ever existed, I did feel it should be mentioned.

After all, if someone has made a deliberate attempt to wipe out the memory of the *SS Ourang Medan*, they must have had some compelling reason to do so. If there was nothing to cover up, then why try to erase the existence of the ship from public records? It was really only luck that a remaining archive in Germany held some information about the vessel, thus luckily providing proof of it having even ever existed.

Now we'll look at a much better documented case, one with photographs of the deceased, as well as many supporting documents from the actual investigations by the Soviet authorities of the time:

The Dyatlov Pass Incident, January, 1959, "A Compelling Unknown Force." This event, which we've referred to in our book, *Darker Side Of The Moon "They" Are Watching Us!* can hardly be referred to as just a mere incident. It is for this reason I include it again here, because it was such a horrifying and major event. The circumstances and number of deaths involved make this so.

The circumstances are truly terrible, like something out of a science fiction horror movie. The facts of the Dyatlov Pass Incident are not just horrifying, but also perplexing. It also is one of the most mysterious events ever recorded, if not the most mysterious of all in some respects.

It all started in 1959, on January 25. A group of young people decided to take a skiing/hiking trip in the Ural Mountain area of the then Soviet Union. There were a number of students, a ski instructor, and three engineers. The students attended the Ural Polytechnic Institute in Sverdlovsk (so named at the time). They decided that this trip should take place in and around the Otorten Mountain area. "Otorten" in English means, literally, "Don't Go There." The local tribes people had given the area the name hundreds or more years ago, and apparently for a good reason, as it turned out.

The team was expert skiers. These weren't novices. The group was led by Igor Dyatlov, and after the incident that was to occur, the mountain pass became known as Dyatlov Pass. The team set out, minus one member, Yury Yudin, who became too sick to make the journey. He remained behind in a small village by the name of Vizhai, literally the last place of civilization before one entered the vast wilderness of the region.

The group set off, enthusiastic about their trip, the chance to get in some cross-country skiing, and just to enjoy the outdoors in general. This was the last time they would be seen alive.

Time passed and nothing was heard of them. People weren't too worried when they didn't make their arrival time, but as more and more time passed, concern mounted. The Ural Polytechnic Institute, at the urging of family members of the students, decided they needed to investigate. They instituted a search.

As even more time passed, days, it was decided such a ground-based search was insufficient. They requested the authorities to lend their aid in a more massive search. This included air as well as more ground-based resources.

The rescuers eventually made their way to *Kholat Syakhl*. Again, this is a local tribal name for a mountain, which translated into English means, "Mountain of the Dead." Again, we have that forbidding sot of name. The Mansi tribes people ranged everywhere, and yet this was an area that from ancient times, they had referred to as a place one shouldn't go, and a place of death.

The search party discovered the tent of the hikers. It was in a bad state, having been partially knocked down and torn. They also discovered the footprints of the hikers all around the tent and immediate area. These showed either the skiers had fled the area in their bare or stocking feet, which meant they had left in a real panic. To go without shoes in subzero conditions was worse than foolhardy.

In addition, despite all this evidence, of the hikers/skiers themselves, there was no sign. They simple seemed to have fled the area leaving everything of value to their survival behind. Again, this seemed to indicate an extreme state of panic on their part to do something so desperate. Moreover, it also seemed to indicate that whatever occurred had occurred very quickly. There were even signs the skiers had cut their way out of the tent in their rush to be free, rather than using the regular entrance/exit.

Determined to find the skiers, the rescuers followed a couple of sets of footprints to a wooded area not far away from the campsite. Here, they came across the remnants of a campfire and the remains of two of the skiers.

An Oddity. Although not far at all from the tent and their belongings, ones they needed to survive such freezing conditions, such as their shoes and warm clothing, the two dead men were naked. Branches on nearby trees had been broken and later, tests showed human skin and flesh was found embedded in the bark. The hands of the dead men showed wounds, ones that seem to have been incurred, inflicted on themselves, in their desperation to climb the trees.

To the rescuers, this seemed indicative of them having tried frantically to avoid an animal attack. However, the footprints of any such a beast were entirely lacking, either by where the men were found, or back by the tent. Yet, human footprints abounded. The mystery grew.

The corpse of Dyatlov was found shortly later, almost a thousand feet from the first two. He lay on his back, a tree limb clutched in one hand. Closer to the tent, another body was found, this one lying face down. This body showed signs of a major head injury. However, death was determined to be the result of his having frozen to death, perhaps while he lay there unconscious, rather than because of that injury.

Later, they found yet another body, that of a young woman, Zinaida Kolmogorov. Although some blood was found near her, she seemed uninjured. Try as they might, the would-be rescuers were unable to ascertain the location of the rest of the skiing party.

All the rescuers could determine for sure is that something terrible had happened, something bizarre, and it had caused the entire skiing party to flee their tent anyway they could, in a frantic hurry and total panic to not even dress or grab warm clothing to take with them. They had run out into the freezing cold with no way to stay warm. They were either naked, under clothed, and/or shoeless, and so exposed to the harsh arctic conditions.

Two months would pass before, with the coming of better weather conditions, the bodies of the remaining cross-country skiers were discovered. However, rather than helping to solve the enigma of what had unfolded, they only seemed to make things even more mysterious. The remaining bodies lay in a gulley not far from where the first two had been located. It seems these last four had died of internal injuries.

Oddly, unlike the others, these four weren't naked, but had their clothes on them, although some seem to have been borrowed from the others. Investigators determined some type of "heavy object" had shattered their skulls, and/or chests. However, despite the fact they might not have perished immediately, there was no bruising to be found on them. A doctor, Borish Vozrozhdenny, upon examination of the bodies said the force was *"equal to the effect of a car crash."* One of the corpses had the tongue removed, as if torn from her mouth.

Again, there was some evidence these refugees were wearing some of the clothing of the others, but how and when they had obtained them, seems uncertain, except that perhaps, while fleeing the tent, they had grabbed whatever they could lying near them, or had later stripped the bodies of their friends. Yet, there was no evidence for this last. Why do this when they could easily have walked back to the tent to get everything they needed and more besides?

Another thing of note is that the relatives of the deceased noticed some of the victims had a distinctly odd orange tint to them. They also said the hair lacked its normal color, had gone gray. Additionally, the corpses had a higher radiation level than was normal, and yet this did not seem to have been the cause of their deaths.

There was a plethora of questions about all this, of course. Besides the obvious ones, as with regard to who or what had killed them, and under what circumstances, were other less obvious ones. These included why an experienced group, headed by the even more experienced Dyatlov, would set up camp in such an exposed area to begin with, one so open to the elements, when there were more sheltered places not far away to be had?

The answer to this question is unknown. Conjectures have been made, such as perhaps they wanted to see if they could manage a camp in so exposed an area, for the sake of practice in an emergency, although, this seems to stretch credulity to think they would do this under such circumstances.

The film in their cameras, once developed did provide some more clues. For example, the photographs all showed normal, healthy individuals, and no sign of problems. Further evidence suggested they made camp at about five o'clock in the evening. Another question is why were so many of the victims naked or virtually so? Who divests themselves of all their clothes when the temperature was very close to, or just below zero degrees Fahrenheit?

Investigations showed that whatever happened, happened after they'd eaten their evening meal. The event seemed to have had to take place around 10:00 PM, or within an hour or so of either side of that time. Something, or someone(s) apparently had so scared the group as a whole, that they had fled the warmth of their tent around that time. They had braved horrible and freezing weather conditions to escape whatever it was that was occurring.

They did this, knowing as experienced cross-country skiers that they couldn't survive long at all under such conditions and in such a state of undress. Still, they fled anyway, even knowing this fact. One thing of note; although footprints showed they'd scattered out into the night, they also showed they had managed to again find each other and apparently, had taken shelter under the trees where the first two bodies had been discovered.

It seems they also had tried to start a fire to stay warm, but they did not attempt to return to the campsite, a place less than 2,000 feet away, to obtain much needed clothing to help insure their survival. Whatever had scared them, kept them from even attempting to go back.

However, later during the night, several, out of desperation, might have tried to return to the campsite to get what they needed, but never made it. "Something" killed them first.

It seems possible the remaining four tried to seek refuge further in the woods, but they, too, met their deaths in some bizarre way. Questions remain to this day. Just what had occurred that terrible night to all those skiers? What killed them?

Animals don't seem a reasonable explanation, since the corpses didn't appear to have been partially eaten at the time the bizarre incident occurred. What was the "heavy object" that caused the trauma without bruising? Why were the bodies more radioactive than was considered normal? What caused the orange skin and gray hair? And most of all, what would cause experienced skiers, so many of them, to panic so thoroughly and flee into terrible and freezing weather conditions, many naked or nearly so, and without any thought of standing their ground and fighting?

Many suppositions as to why or how have been proposed to explain all this, but none of them seem to work well. Some said a possible avalanche could have caused their flight. If so, where was the evidence of such a thing having happened? Why wouldn't they go back to the campsite right afterwards to get what they needed? Even if another avalanche might have been in the offing, they would have had little choice. It was either retrieve what they needed or die.

The idea natives might have murdered them seems equally ludicrous. Remember how many of the skiers there were, how healthy and young they were. Surely, some would have stood their ground, have battled to survive. Moreover, what would the local tribes people being doing out under such adverse conditions, and so far from any nearby village or dwellings? Such solutions simply don't seem to explain the circumstances of the event.

One other note here; the area was then closed to skiers for several years, out of fear, presumably, of such a thing happening to other would-be cross-country skiers. The authorities were worried. There was something more to consider, as well—UFOs.

At the same time this dreadful event happened, other hikers spotted what they described as "strange orange spheres" in the sky to their north. Since they were approximately 32 miles south of the murdered skiers, and these lights were to their north, it puts the UFOs near the skiers, right at the time the events took place. Moreover, over the next two months, others in the region observed such UFOs, as well. Even members of the military, along with civilians, spotted such UFOs.

When one of the investigators, Lev Ivanov, suspected, based on this information, that UFOs/aliens might be the cause of the deaths, the Soviet authorities summarily ordered the case closed, the files on it classified. In an interview much later, he stated he was commanded to keep secret the information about the UFOs and other aspects of the case. However, he also stated:

"I suspected at the time, and am almost sure now, that these bright flying spheres had a direct connection to the group's death."

It is odd that the removal of the one student's tongue so closely resembles cattle mutilations today. The tongue is one of the parts of cattle and animals in such mutilations that are commonly removed. He also points to the low but significant level of radiation of the bodies.

One thing is certain in all of this, people died horrible deaths under the most bizarre circumstances and UFOs were sighted repeatedly in the immediate area.

Furthermore, the area seems to have been considered dangerous and "forbidden" by the local inhabitants for an incredibly long time. So long, in fact, did they feel this, that major features of the region had acquired dire names as warnings to stay away from them. Is it just an accident this event occurred in an area named "don't go there," on "the mountain of the dead?" If so, it is yet another weird aspect of all this.

In any case, Lev Ivanov concluded in his report that *"an unknown elemental force which they were unable to overcome"* killed the skiers. Was this "elemental force" something to do with UFOs?

Well, considering every other theory, and there are lots of them, including even the idea of a yeti or abominable snowman (but no footprints found of such) fails to adequately explain what happened, UFOs seem the most likely cause. Because, for instance, if there had been an avalanche, there should have been evidence of such, snow having buried the tent or at least piles of the stuff should have been nearby.

If murderous tribes people were the cause, where are their footprints, and how did they kill people with the force of a "car" crash but not leave any bruising? If radiation from some secret weapon and/or military event was the cause, why the missing tongue of the one woman, or the bodies found naked when there were clothes at the campsite some 1,500 yards away? Why are there no footprints of soldiers who may have killed them to silence them? Why are some stripped, but not others? If an abominable snowman (Yeti) was the cause, again, why are there no footprints of such a creature either, when there are plenty of the skiers? Why the gray hair and orange skin of some of the bodies?

No, there seems only one real answer to all of this. This isn't just out of any preference on my part, either, but simply as a process of elimination, because it is the only explanation left that seems to fit all the available facts. Those "glowing orange spheres," UFOs, were in the area and right at the time of the horrible tragedy. Is this just a weird coincidence? Terrible, bizarre deaths and UFOs sighted nearby and there is no connection? Such beggars one's ability to believe this, if so.

In any case, nine young people died horrible and strange deaths. Only one survived, because he had felt too ill (and it is said had an ominous premonition, as well), and so did not take that leg of the journey with them.

UFOs seem to have been the culprits or in some way involved. Worse, whatever happened seemed to have not just attacked them, but also then hunted them down after the initial assault. So if UFOs or the occupants of them perpetrated this horror, it shows that deaths can and do result from them. UFOs are dangerous it seems, sometimes fatally so. We aren't done with those mysterious orange spheres yet. I will discuss more cases involving them later on.

Death of Twenty-Year Old Australian Pilot, 1978. Frederick Valentich, a young civilian pilot in Australia had a fatal encounter with a UFO(s). Another thing here; this is a crossover incident, since not only is the pilot presumed long dead now, but also he and his plane disappeared without a trace. Therefore, this case could just as easily be included in our disappearance section of the book.

Frederick was flying over the Bass Strait along the coast of Victoria, Australia. His destination was King Island. Then he informed the Melbourne Air Traffic Control that he was encountering lights, four of them, approximately 1,000 feet above his position. As he described them and their bizarre behavior, the lights could only be UFOs.

Nor was he alone in these sightings. There were twenty other witnesses in different locations in the greater area who claimed to have spotted what they thought were UFOs, so his reporting such a thing is well corroborated by others, as well. The eyewitness reports seem to describe elongated objects, one describing it as a "sky rocket," although it didn't seem to be moving. Another described a "cigar" shape. There were other reports. One set of witnesses thought the object was "star shaped," and others just reported weird lights in the sky.

Frederick continued to speak with the control tower, reporting what he was seeing. He became more agitated after a while, claimed the lights were buzzing him and getting too close. Then, all communication ceased. The young Frederick, along with plane, vanished, never to be seen again, although one witness in Apollo Bay reportedly saw the plane go down near Cape Marengo. A young girl who asked him what the light in the sky was, had drawn his attention to this. He responded by saying it was a plane, but she countered by saying she was referring to another light above the plane.

This information wasn't made general knowledge until the Herald-Sun of Melbourne, Australia reported it in October, 2000. What's more, the witness hadn't actually seen the plane crash, but rather he saw it disappear behind some hills that lay in that direction.

Again, neither Frederick nor his plane was ever heard of again, although the craft, a Cessna, did have a survival beacon. Still, this seems to have mysteriously failed, because no trace of a signal was ever received.

As for the control tower recording of the flight, as so often seems to be the case in these incidents, was partially erased, although how, or why, is unknown. This means no resolution was ever to be made with regard to a strange noise heard right near the end of Frederick Valentich's frantic messages, a noise as of metal rubbing on metal. This noise had caused the controller to ask Valentich several times what the source of the sound was. Also Frederick's last words were deleted, as well, in which he said there was fire shooting from a cylinder-like craft as it flew directly above him. He said his Cessna was surrounded by an aura or greenish glow, and that he felt as if he were burning. This is when all contact with Frederick ceased.

Please note that sensation of "burning" mentioned above. This seems to be a common thing for witnesses to describe. It often forms a common thread in many UFO incidents reported by witnesses and victims of UFO encounters.

The main portion of the actual recorded transcript of the conversation between Frederick Valentich and the Melbourne Air Traffic Controller (Melbourne Flight Service, referred to in the transcript as "DSJ Melbourne, and Frederick's plane as "Delta Sierra Juliet") did survive. It is included here, so that readers can judge for themselves the nature of the event:

TRANSCRIPT:

"19:06:14 DSJ Melbourne, this is Delta Sierra Juliet. Is there any known traffic below five thousand?

FS Delta Sierra Juliet, no known traffic.

DSJ Delta Sierra Juliet, I am, seems to be a large aircraft below five thousand.

19:06:44 FS Delta Sierra Juliet, What type of aircraft is it?

DSJ Delta Sierra Juliet, I cannot affirm, it is four bright, and it seems to me like landing lights.

19:07 FS Delta Sierra Juliet.

19:07:31 DSJ Melbourne, this is Delta Sierra Juliet, the aircraft has just passed over me at least a thousand feet above.

FS Delta Sierra Juliet, roger, and it is a large aircraft, confirmed?

DSJ Er-unknown, due to the speed it's traveling, is there any air force aircraft in the vicinity?

FS Delta Sierra Juliet, no known aircraft in the vicinity.

19:08:18 DSJ Melbourne, it's approaching now from due east towards me.

FS Delta Sierra Juliet.

19:08:41 DSJ (open microphone for two seconds.)

19:08:48 DSJ Delta Sierra Juliet, it seems to me that he's playing some sort of game, he's flying over me two, three times at speeds I could not identify.

19:09 FS Delta Sierra Juliet, roger, what is your actual level?

DSJ My level is four and a half thousand, four five zero zero.

FS Delta Sierra Juliet and you confirm you cannot identify the aircraft?

DSJ Affirmative.

FS Delta Sierra Juliet, roger, stand by.

19:09:27 DSJ Melbourne, Delta Sierra Juliet, it's not an aircraft it is (open microphone for two seconds).

19:09:42 FS Delta Sierra Juliet, can you describe the - ER- aircraft?

DSJ Delta Sierra Juliet, as it's flying past it's a long shape (open microphone for three seconds) cannot identify more than it has such speed (open microphone for three seconds). It's before me right now Melbourne.

19:10 FS Delta Sierra Juliet, roger and how large would the - er - object be?

19:10:19 DSJ Delta Sierra Juliet, Melbourne, it seems like it's stationary. What I'm doing right now is orbiting and the thing is just orbiting on top of me also. It's got a green light and sort of metallic like, it's all shiny on the outside.

FS Delta Sierra Juliet

19:10:46 DSJ Delta Sierra Juliet (open microphone for three seconds) It's just vanished.

FS Delta Sierra Juliet

19:11 DSJ Melbourne, would you know what kind of aircraft I've got? Is it a military aircraft?

FS Delta Sierra Juliet, Confirm the - er ~ aircraft just vanished.

DSJ Say again.

FS Delta Sierra Juliet, is the aircraft still with you?

DSJ Delta Sierra Juliet; it's (open microphone for two seconds) now approaching from the south-west.

FS Delta Sierra Juliet

1911:50 DSJ Delta Sierra Juliet, the engine is rough-idling. I've got it set at twenty three twenty-four and the thing is coughing.

FS Delta Sierra Juliet, roger, what are your intentions?

DSJ My intentions are - ah - to go to King Island - ah - Melbourne. That strange aircraft is hovering on top of me again (open microphone for two seconds). It is hovering and it's not an aircraft.

FS Delta Sierra Juliet.

1912:28 DSJ Delta Sierra Juliet. Melbourne (open microphone for seventeen seconds).

(An unexplained sound abruptly terminated the voice communications.)"

Also, following, is a portion of the official Associate Press report on this tragic incident:

ASSOCIATED PRESS ANNOUNCEMENT:
Source: AP MELBOURNE, AUSTRALIA.
Date: October 25, 1978.
AUSTRALIAN PILOT DISAPPEARS AFTER REPORTING CHASE BY UFO'S:

Boats and aircraft have found no trace of the 20-year old Australian pilot who disappeared with his plane on Saturday night after radioing that he was being chased by a UFO. Frederick Valentich was on a 125 mile training flight in his single engine Cessna 182 along the coast of Bass Strait when he told air traffic controllers in Melbourne that he was being buzzed by a UFO with 4 bright lights about 1000 feet above him.

Controllers said his last message was taped and was: "It's approaching from due east towards me. It seems to be playing some sort of game... flying at a speed I can't estimate. It's not an aircraft. It's...It is flying past. It is a long shape. I cannot identify more than that. It's coming for me right now." A minute later: "It seems to be stationary. I'm also orbiting and the thing is orbiting on top of me also. It has a green light and a sort of metallic light on the outside." Valentich then radioed that his engine was running roughly. His last words were: "It is not an aircraft."

CONCLUSION: Just what was it that Valentich saw, and which ultimately made him and his plane seemingly disappear from the face of the Earth forever? Well, to quote again his last words *"It is not an aircraft."* Therefore, if it wasn't one of ours, but there was something there, and by his repeated descriptions, it wasn't something naturally occurring, therefore, by logical default, it had to be "one of theirs." And by "theirs," I mean extraterrestrial.

Of course, it would help if we could interview Valentich about all this now, but that's impossible, because chances are, he is (1) dead, and in any case, alive or dead, he is (2) disappeared. It would seem this is a permanent condition for him, sadly and unfortunately. Moreover, by the transcription recording, it hardly seems it was an accident.

CHAPTER 8—MILITARY DEATHS RELATED TO UFOS

"It is my thesis that flying saucers are real and that they are space ships from another solar system. There is no doubt in my mind that these objects are interplanetary craft of some sort."
—**Dr. Herman Oberth**

We have discussed injuries to military personnel involved in UFO sightings, but the deadly problem goes further than this, and seems to have been doing so for some long time now. Besides civilians dying, so are members of various countries' armed forces. Below, are just a few examples of these fatal phenomena. I will start with perhaps the first and most famous case of such a death:

Lt. Felix Moncla Jr. and Second Lt. Robert Wilson, November 1953. Two military pilots flew into oblivion on this date. Neither they nor their plane was ever seen again. This is a classic case in the annals of UFO history. It is also one of the earliest ones. With regard to a military death, it is considered by many to be the very first one.

Therefore, many people may already be aware of this particular incident. I repeat it here to establish the fact of the time of the beginning of such deaths for military personnel with regard to UFOs.

Lieutenant Felix Moncla was at Truax Field in Madison, Wisconsin. However, the powers-that-be had decided to transfer him on a temporary basis to the Kinross Air Force Base. This was in the Upper Peninsula of Michigan.

November 23, 1953, Lieutenant Moncla and second Lieutenant Wilson flew on a mission to investigate an unidentified object. It had penetrated restricted airspace. This was near the So Locks area, close to the Canadian border. Neither officer was a novice at flying, with Moncla having over 1000 hours of flying time by this point. Their jet was state-of-the-art for the time, being an F-89C. This meant that they could fly at high speeds, even by today's standards. Traveling at approximately 500 miles per hour as they flew at an altitude of 7000 feet, they approached the UFO. At around 8,000 feet, they closed with the object.

Even before they established visual contact, a radar operator located in Houghton, Michigan had the object on his scope. He watched as the jet closed with the UFO. The two objects seemed to merge on the screen. After that, there was only one object left, and it shot off the radar screen, traveling to the north and into Canadian territory. Of the two pilots and their jet, nothing was ever seen or found. It was as if they and their jet had simply vanished forever.

Of course, search teams were mounted and sent out. They scoured the Lake Superior area, specifically the region where the plane was last seen on radar. Their efforts were fruitless.

As time passed, explanations for what happened came and went. At first, they presumed the plane might have gone down because of weather conditions. Although the weather wasn't the best that night, it wasn't extreme by any means, either. The likelihood of the plane going down for such a reason seemed almost impossibly slim. In any case, again, there was no mayday signal from them.

Then, as seems inevitable with these cases, the military began to backtrack on what it had previously divulged to the public. Although it first having publicly said the two objects had merged on the radarscope and the Associated Press had published the account this way, they recanted their statement, and said that had not happened. Furthermore, they tried to say the UFO was, in actuality, a Canadian jet. Canada denied this, said it had no aircraft in the area at the time the event had occurred, and so in no way was any of their aircraft involved.

The next thing the Air Force said was that Lieutenant Moncla could well have been the victim of vertigo. This might have caused him to lose control of the plane and have it then plummet down into the lake. They stated that Moncla had suffered from vertigo on several prior occasions. Really?

This statement was ludicrous on the face of it. Any pilot in the military who suffered from such an illness to the extent it might cause him to crash an expensive jet never would have flown in the first place. They would have summarily retired him from commanding or flying any aircraft. This was standard procedure.

Investigator Gordon Heath claims the communications officer had clearly heard the lieutenant after his plane had supposedly disappeared, had merged with the other radar blip, as if it were still flying and so okay. Therefore, the idea the plane had already crashed into the lake by that point, just does not work very well, either.

So just what did happen to those two men and their jet? Well, it is possible they could have crashed into the lake, of course. However, if they had done so, it would have been at high speed. The jet should have shattered, as such craft do under such high velocity conditions. Furthermore, why didn't the pilots radio in with a mayday message if this was the case? This didn't happen, either. Nor was the yet seen falling off the radar screen.

At some point, after some time, some of the wreckage and/or debris should have washed up on shore or been found somewhere. Although the wreckage of a plane was found much later, years in fact, it was determined these were not the remains of Moncla's jet, but another type of craft entirely.

Again, the authorities never discovered any wreckage of the plane. No bodies ever turned up. Even after 62 years, the better part of a century, not a single piece of debris from the jet has become known. Again, somewhere, somehow, if the plane had crashed into the lake, some small pieces of it should have washed up somewhere. This was not the case then, and the better part of a century, is still not the case.

Moreover, the U.S. Air Force would not declare Moncla and Wilson dead for over another month after the time of the incident. This seemed to imply they didn't think the two men were dead. Yet, if the plane had crashed and the men had never radioed in, and no bodies were found, surely after just a week or so of searching, the men should have been declared dead? Why the long delay on the Air Force's part in doing this?

Furthermore, they never held a memorial for either of the men. This is out of character for the Air Force and in fact, is distinctly odd. It is a matter of standard procedure eventually to hold such a memorial service for any fallen comrades. This never happened.

The plane and men had simply vanished, apparently forever. In Moreauville, at the Catholic Cemetery there, a memorial simply says the men had intercepted a UFO and then they had disappeared.

Of course, the question remains, to where did they disappear? Are they truly dead? Well, after 62 years, it would seem likely they may well be. Nevertheless and regardless of whether or not they are still alive, exactly where they vanished to is still a big question.

Some Clues. There are some interesting clues. Remember, the radar operator said the two blips on his scope seeming to merge into one. He then said the one took off to the north and eventually disappeared from his screen. Then we had that communications officer who claimed to have heard Moncla speak, and this was after the time of the supposed crash of the jet and/or the merging of the two blips. This means that at that time, Moncla and most likely, Wilson, were not dead, at least, not yet.

So what does that leave us? Well, there is only one real answer left. If the two blips merged into one, if the men were still alive after this occurred, and then the blip moved away at high speed, the jet must have gone with it. This means the plane must have been inside the object. Therefore, the UFO abducted the two crewmembers and their craft. This is very much like what seems to have happened to Frederick Valentich in his Cessna while flying over the Bass Strait, Australia.

The truth is that one can only make conjectures, even if reasonable ones given the available facts. We may never know what happened to those two men and their jet. There really seems to be no way of finding out now, except to scour the lakebed of Lake Superior in the hopes of finding the remains of the crashed plane. Perhaps, someday this will happen.

Even then, it would beg the question of why it happened. That there was a UFO sighted can be no doubt. That they and their jet had been launched to intercept it, is also in no doubt. That it was not a Canadian aircraft is also no longer in question.

Whatever happened, it can only be one of two things: either their jet was made to crash and disappear into the lake forever, or they were abducted. Either way, their encounter with a UFO had deadly repercussions for them. For their family and friends there never would be closure. To this day, they wonder what happened to their loved ones.

Deaths Of Soviet Divers, 1982. Major General Demyanko, of the Soviet Union's Ministry of Defense, and the commander of the Military Diver Service, informed the commanders of an ongoing training exercise for divers at the Issik Kul Lake to be careful. The reason he cited for this warning astonished them. Major Demyanko explained that at recent and similar exercises at Lake Baikal, divers with that group had discovered something momentous and very dangerous, at least to them.

The divers, while performing their part in the exercises sighted other swimmers. The odd part about this encounter was that despite the depths the Russian divers were at; these "swimmers" were not wearing any of the standard types of scuba gear. They did wear "silvery suits" and "helmets." Who they were, what they were doing there was a mystery. This was part of Soviet Russia. Whoever they were, they didn't belong, didn't have authorization to be in those waters.

Those higher up, decided the Russian divers should attempt to intercept and detain one of these silver-suited figures. The divers attempted to do so. As they swam toward the strangers, they fled, swimming swiftly away from them.

The recounting of this episode says that at one point, the divers tried to net one of the silver swimmers. This resulted in disastrous consequences. Something or some power erupted from the depths just below them, forcing them up and to the surface. Without taking the appropriate time to allow their bodies to adjust to the sudden drop in pressure on them, they all suffered a case of the "bends." The symptoms are dramatic and often deadly. Rapid decompression, gas bubbles, which can rapidly form just about anywhere in the body is the result.

This causes extreme pain. Agony, might be a better description for it, as well as often causing paralysis, and even excruciating death. The term, "the bends" comes from the fact that when such gas bubbles form in the joints, it causes the victim to contort, bend over, and sometimes assume a complete fetal position. Again, the suffering involved in this is extreme, excruciating beyond belief. In other words, if you had to pick a way to die, this certainly would not be one of the easier ways to go!

This happened to the Russian divers. Moreover, the best treatment for this sort of rapid decompression illness is hyperbaric oxygen therapy in a recompression chamber, which creates the same pressure conditions as the divers were originally at in the depths of the water. Then they slowly change the pressure back to atmospheric normal over hours, and sometimes, even days.

However, there was a problem. There was only one useable pressure chamber nearby. It could hold only two people. The commander, trying to do his best for his men, jammed four into the chamber. The results of this were catastrophic. Three of the divers ultimately died and the survivors all became permanently handicapped, severely so.

How does this connect with UFOs? Well, actually in this case, I am talking about USOs (Unidentified Submerged Objects). Large disk-shaped craft had been seen in the depths of Lake Baikal, as well as Sarez Lake, a very deep reservoir not far from there. At the reservoir, the Soviets had repeatedly tracked "disc-like" craft, even capturing them surfacing and taking off into the skies.

In addition, creatures similar to the ones the Russian divers had encountered were seen, complete with being in silver suits. This was in the same waters, often close to the times of the sighting of the underwater discs or submerged "spheres" as some witnesses described them.

More importantly, the Soviet military declared all information pertaining to this subject, the encounters, sightings, and the reason for the Russian divers' deaths and injuries, as classified.

An important thing to note here is how many divers there were involved in this encounter. These were all military professionals, had much experience in their chosen profession, and all of them, every man knew the dangers of rapid decompression. They understood the terrible results it could produce. It is one of the biggest fears all such types of divers have, that along with deprivation of their air when submerged so far below the surface of the water.

This means that none of them, not one, would have simply swam to the surface in such a hurry, not under any conditions, and certainly not knowing the horrible deaths they would face if they did so. Something forced them to the surface against their will. They had no choice, because if they had been given one, they certainly would not have willingly committed such an agonizing form of attempted suicide. Such an idea would be preposterous in the extreme.

No, something, some "power" forced them upwards to the surface, and some poor men paid with their lives, others with permanent disabilities. "Something" caused this, and it wasn't human in nature. Moreover, it was connected to strange creatures in weird diving gear, and the multiple sightings of UFOs and USOs on several occasions and near the time this event occurred.

To put it succinctly, the divers died or became permanently crippled due to an interaction with a UFO/USO and through no fault of their own. This much seems self-evident.

We have seen in this chapter how even members of our military, as well as those of other countries, die in some UFO encounters. So not only are civilians subject to deaths in such situations, but even our fighting forces seem powerless to survive at times. Whether in jets, on land, or in the sea, members of the military can and do die at times from encounters with UFOs. This adds to the growing body of evidence that UFOs are dangerous, sometimes, deadly dangerous.

CHAPTER 9—DEATHS OF INVESTIGATORS &RESEARCHERS

"The least improbable explanation is that these things are artificial and controlled ... My opinion for some time has been that they have an extraterrestrial origin."
—Dr. Maurice Biot

People die. They die all the time and in all sorts of ways, some ways being worse than others are, as we have already shown in this book. For example, the Soviet divers certainly had an excruciating form of death, one that was a terrible form of torture with their fatal cases of the bends.

However, usually, deaths occur in "normal" ways, whether people dying in a car, train, or plain wreck, or of "natural causes," such as fatal strokes and heart attacks, cancer, etc. Whatever the cause(s), these are expected things. The case of the soviet divers, as with others mentioned in this book, simply does not fall into this category of the expected.

Yes, one can die of the bends if they surface too quickly from too far down in the water, and divers around the world have had this happen to them, but usually the cause of this isn't some "unknown force" driving them to the surface against their wishes, and while they are chasing down weird suited creatures underwater. As we've also shown, sometimes, UFOs kill people.

This, in itself, is bizarre enough. However, in the case of UFO investigators and researchers, as well as some journalists and others, something else very extraordinary seems to be going on, as well. Not only have the researchers and UFO investigators been dying, but the statistics concerning their deaths are strange. They tell a frightening story.

It seems many researchers, and/or scientists investigating UFOs are dying under very doubtful circumstances. In fact, one could almost say that at certain times, they were "popping off" in droves! One would have to assume this is not out of sympathy for others of their brethren who have died at the time, but for some other reason. That seems a very bizarre reason, if so.

Again, the deaths seem to defy the statistical norms, with many dying from heart attacks and cancers too often, and too often at a very young age. This is not normal. Heart diseases advance with one's age, so older people are far more likely to die of heart-related illnesses than younger people are.

Yes, there are aberrations in this, as with all things. This is to be expected. Yet, the statistics regarding the deaths of researchers are directly contrary to this pattern, defy this idea and to such a degree as to cause notice by many. The deaths of so many people under such circumstances are more than just a statistical aberration. It is a cause for alarm.

That's not all. Many have died by supposed suicide (and utilizing some very weird methods to commit such acts, as well), with some using poison, some being shot, some strangled, self-electrocuted, and the list in this regard goes on. Nor is this a new phenomenon. It's been going on for decades.

Inexplicable and yes, frankly suspicious deaths of researchers in the UFO field, are nothing new. As far back as 1971, this topic has caused interest and consternation. For instance, Otto Binder wrote an in-depth article. His, *Liquidation of the UFO Investigators* came out that year in ***Saga***.

It was the author's conclusion in this article for the magazine that many people connected with researching the UFO phenomenon had died and under odd conditions. In his opinion, he felt there were at least 137 such researchers, investigators into the UFO phenomenon, as well as those who witnessed certain UFO events, who died in just one ten-year period alone. He felt these deaths were often under strange and unusual conditions.

The opinion there have been such strange deaths isn't limited to just one or two people, either. Timothy Hood, one-time advisor to the US government, has said much the same thing. At an Amsterdam conference in the Netherlands, he pointed out there had been an alarming number of mysterious deaths throughout the decades of the 1970s and 1980s. Mr. Hood based this belief of his on no less than 30 years of diligent research into the matter.

This phenomenon hasn't stopped. Although Mr. Binder was talking about the deaths of researchers of UFOs in the 1960's, they still seem to be happening to this very day. Now this part is crucial to our way of thinking; the deaths of just so many researchers/scientists somehow or some way involved with UFOs seems incredibly high and has been an ongoing thing since the late 1940s. Just how has this been happening and to whom? Well, this book lists a number of them below.

This is rather a lengthy list, and not just a quick "representative" sample of cases, as I have done with s topics here. The reason I am including so many, but certainly not all, is to give the reader a real feel for just how far reaching, how extensive these deaths have been. Not only are they numerous, but they have been going on for decades. They seem to have started not long after the Roswell Incident in New Mexico. Moreover, I wanted to drive home the point how so many of the deaths seem to have been under mysterious circumstances.

Deaths:

Secretary Of Defense Under President Truman, James Forrestal. Let's start at the beginning. This one, UFO buffs have all heard of, but it does seem to be the start of suspicious death, so I'm including it here.

Forrestal supposedly jumped from a window on the sixteenth floor of the Bethesda Naval Hospital. This occurred in April 1949. President Truman was in power at the time.

Said to have been the victim of some type of emotional or mental breakdown, Secretary of Defense, James Forrestal, resigned his position suddenly and without warning. Subsequently, he entered the Bethesda Hospital, and given a private room there, complete with security. This, in itself, seems strange, since no longer a member of the government, what was he doing at a facility reserved for government officials?

Up until his supposed nervous collapse, Forrestal had only received the highest praise for his abilities and endeavors throughout his entire career. He had even made the cover of **Time Magazine** while still Secretary of Defense. His, had been a long, sound, and solid career. World War II had been no problem for the man, for instance, and instead, he had excelled in his various governmental positions during that time.

Nevertheless, at the time of his supposed "breakdown," which seemed to have occurred unbelievably quickly, he summarily left office (via his resignation, which many consider a forced one by the President) and went to the hospital. This was purportedly against his wishes, for some claimed he was afraid to go, feared what might happen to him once there. The "official" reason for his admittance to the hospital was "operational fatigue." This is a vague term at best and tells us little.

Some of his family claim they were denied admittance to see him and it does seem he was kept incommunicado, in virtual isolated confinement, except for a select group, and those not chosen by him. "They" (whoever the higher-ups in charge of him were) denied him certain visitors he had requested, again, even certain members of his own family, including his brother. Yet, weirdly, other ones came to see him in private and these had far less reason to do so. Or so one would think.

He had been visited by not only his wife and sons, who it was claimed he was not close to, but also by Sidney Souers, who was once an NSC executive secretary, and who also has been claimed to have been a member of that notorious UFO secret government group, MJ- (or "MAJESTIC") 12. Once more, despite having received other such peculiar visitors, Forrestal was denied his requests (and even theirs, in the case of his brother, for instance) to see the ones he most wanted to have visit. This included not only his brother, but also two priests, ones he counted as his friends.

At last, permission was given for his brother to visit the next day, but by then, Forrestal was already dead, having been found on a thirteenth floor roof with a cord wrapped around his neck.

Questions abound about his death. Even the most hardened and skeptical investigators often refer to it as "peculiar" with regard to the circumstances involved. However, I simply don't have room here for what could be a book-length dissertation about Secretary Forrestal alone. There is that much to be said about it all, but here are the highlights:

That Forrestal was high up in government, well regarded by many as a brilliant and an accomplished man is a fact. That they suddenly rushed him to the hospital after vague rumors surfaced about his mental health, and then there denied those he wanted particularly to see admittance, is also a matter of record. That this refusal included religious visitors he'd specifically requested is unusual, indeed.

Why his spiritual counselors had their visitations denied, despite repeated requests on Forrestal's part, as well as theirs, with the reason given that it was an "inopportune" time is just bizarre. Yet, others visited him, including a congressman?

Since when are chaplains refused admittance to see the ill at hospitals? What was repeatedly so "inopportune" as to deny such visits of comfort and solace from them, but not from a congressman? Again, this was all very bizarre.

Was the reason Forrestal might have had something to tell them in confession and the government didn't want him to divulge to them what he knew about UFOs? After all, there had to be some reason to deny him spiritual guidance when he was going through such troubled times, but allowing others (a supposed member of MJ-12 being one of them), to visit him.

Why they found Forrestal with a bathrobe cord wound around his neck after having fallen multiple stories to land on the thirteenth floor roof of a neighboring building is just as peculiar. How had he "accidentally" managed to get out of a window with security screening on it also seems very strange. Couldn't he decide which form of suicide he preferred; strangulation or a death by a long fall? Did he try to do both? Had he tried to hang himself and somehow then defeated the security screening of the window and fallen out of it? Alternatively, was he silenced—permanently and on purpose?

There is one thing more. Secretary Forrestal was supposed also to have been a member of MJ-12, and one of the few reported civilians in the group. Rumor had it that he did not like or care for anything about the group or the people composing it. Forrestal didn't get along with any of them, allegedly, and felt there was too much power concentrated too much in the hands of too few.

Worse, these were military people, at that, which as a civilian; Forrestal was supposed to have adamantly feared even more as a result. He was alleged to have felt there power could know no bounds under such circumstances, having such little (if any) oversight as they did of their group.

Then, Forrestal suddenly died. He died under very mysterious circumstances. The whole incident never could have been so easily glossed over, so quickly disposed of publicly today, as it was in the late 1940s. Nowadays, media investigationsand their cry for government investigations would be rampant and extreme.

Or would they? Our media still seems to have a strong predilection for ridiculing the whole UFO phenomenon and everything related to it. One almost never sees a commentator on television mention a UFO sighting without also giving the audience a knowing smirk, a disbelieving raised eyebrow, or an outright smile or even a dismissive chuckle.

The clear message the commentator is delivering? To believe in such things is to be "on the fringe," or perhaps even a little mentally "off." The message does get across with repeating. People often don't report sightings as a result. So even today, the concept of the "Big Lie," or in this case, an unrelenting ridicule does work to silence people, act to shut them up even before they open their mouths.

Even so, the weird circumstances surrounding the death of a Secretary of Defense today would certainly give rise to many questions in the media. One can't see how it would fail to. At least, so one hopes...but perhaps times haven't changed as much as we would like to think with regard to this subject.

Dorothy Kilgallen. Many people have never heard of Dorothy Kilgallen. Yet, MS Kilgallen was a journalist, and a highly renowned one of her day, if not the *most* renowned. While in the United Kingdom on assignment during the period of 1954 to 1955, she sent two "special" communications home to the United States. The first she sent in February of 1954. This missive concerned a special "hush-hush" meeting of various high-ranking military officers from around the world.

The second missive sent the following year, 1955, quoted a member of the British Government's Cabinet, who said:

"I believe, on the basis of our inquiry thus far, that saucers were staffed by small men-probably under four feet tall. It's frightening, but there is no denying the flying saucers come from another planet."

Within days after sending this communication, MS Kilgallen died, supposedly of an overdose of barbiturates and alcohol. Thus, ended her career, and at a time when she seemed involved in a truly momentous story. No doubt, if the story had broken publicly, it could have been the story of the century, or even of the entire history of the world.

So suicide, especially so close to the filing of this latest dispatch, seemed extraordinary, even at the time. Who was the person who leaked this information to her? Rumors say it was the Earl of Mountbatten, no less. However, this aspect of the affair is unverified. That her death was suspicious and the timing of it even more so, is without a doubt.

Furthermore, it was only a year earlier that the so-called Roberson Panel (supposedly a group created by the CIA) is said to have recommended strong and strict enforcement of the cover-up of all things UFO. Suppression of it all, they felt was paramount. Furthermore, they allegedly did not discount any means to accomplish this.

Was MS Kilgallen just another loose cannon in this particular regard? Were her reports the sounding of her death knell as a means of suppression? Furthermore, did she have "help" with regard to her suicide? It certainly came at a propitious time for those wishing to cover up anything about UFOs, since it stopped her further investigating and/or reporting on the topic. However, this was just one of many such bizarre deaths. There are many, many more.

M.K Jessup, Astronomer. In 1959, Mr. Jessup supposedly committed suicide. His work included *The Case for the UFO*, among others. Moreover, he was an astronomer, as well as something of an archaeologist, besides being an author. His death took place in Florida, in Dade County Park.

There is some question as to the cause of his demise, despite his having indicated to others he was in a state of depression, because his state of mind seemed influenced by a "series of strange events," as Ivan Sanderson later put it. Did he become mentally unbalanced? Yes, it would seem so, but it also seems those "strange events" contrived to drive him into such a state.

MS Ann Genzlinger, who thoroughly researched the events and facts leading up to Jessup's death concluded, *"He was under some sort of control."* As a side note, Ivan Sanderson is now long dead, as well, although his death seems to have been a more "normal" one. We use the word "normal" advisedly here.

Remember that at the time, the government didn't mind experimenting with mind-altering drugs, such as LSD, and even using them on unsuspecting victims. (One could hardly call them "subjects," since some seemed to have no choice in the matter and were even unaware that someone was experimenting on them.) It was her belief something like this, at least along these lines, might have been a factor in Jessup's death, although such experiments were kept as a deep secret at the time.

Other factors seem to make this an odd case, as well.

1. Despite the circumstances of his death, there was no autopsy.

2. The style of his death seemed too perfect, or as one put it: *"Everything seemed too professional."*

3. Minor details, even such things as the hose used to funnel exhaust into the car having been wired into position, showed a meticulous concern that is out of the ordinary in such cases.

4. He died at a time when the traffic was heavy, at rush hour, when any of a number of cars streaming by should have noticed something was wrong, especially if there was bumper-to-bumper traffic and they were going slow.

5. His spouse indicated he had been receiving "strange" telephone calls in the days leading up to his demise; and

6. There is also strong reason to believe that the Office of Naval Investigation may have been in contact with him, according to some of those involved in the events of the time. Why was the ONI involved? Reports say Mr. Jessup was researching the so-called Philadelphia Experiment at the time and that he had been in contact with Carlo Allende, *the* prominent figure involved in claiming the existence of such an experiment.

Death Or Disappearance Of Dr. B. Noel Opan. After claiming a confrontation/visit with the so-called Men In Black in 1959, Dr. B. Noel Opan disappeared, apparently forever. One can only surmise he may have died. If not, he went into a very permanent sort of hiding, and a very successful one, as well, because nobody ever discovered his whereabouts after that. What happened to him? Why did he claim a confrontation with the Men In Black? To where did he disappear, if not into death?

Death Or Disappearance Of Investigator Of UFOs, Australian, Edgar Jarrold. He, too, disappeared. This was in 1960 and very close to the time of Dr. Opan's mysterious vanishing. Moreover, Jarrold's cryptic disappearance, just like Opan's, was also of the "permanent" variety, it seems. Is he dead? Well, it would seem more likely than not at this point. Just when he died is the matter at question. Was it at the time of his disappearance? It could well have been.

John Murphy. December 9, 1965, an unknown (UFO) object crashed near the little town of Kecksburg, Pennsylvania. As most of us know, from the outset, things went strangely. The military arrived, members of different branches, and in large numbers. This is according to many of the citizens of Kecksburg who witnessed the event, as well as visitors there at the time.

The military sealed off the area of the purported "crash" and later, a large truck bearing something covered in a tarpaulin, left a under heavy military escort. Accounts of the object that crashed are singularly consistent by most of the witnesses. They all describe a metallic object, "acorn-shaped," and with strange hieroglyphics embossed on its surface.

Moreover, there is considerable evidence something did crash there, that a large number of military personnel were involved, and that the military had sealed off the area. The newspaper, the *Tribune-Review* of Greensburg, a town close to Kecksburg, also covered the event. Their article the following day had the headline:

"Unidentified Flying Object Falls near Kecksburg — Army Ropes off Area". It further stated that: *"The area where the object landed was immediately sealed off on the order of U.S. Army and State Police officials..."*

After that, all coverage to any real extent ended, with a small statement later on in the same paper saying they had found nothing of any significance. Later, the government said the object had only been a meteorite and they had sent only three military members to check it out and ascertain what, if anything, was there.

Yet, nobody has ever shown any fragments of a meteorite. So what had crashed there? If a meteorite, why didn't some university or someone at some point show these meteorite fragments, put them on display, or even mention them, at least? Nothing like this has happened and it's been decades now.

The fact something came to Earth near Kecksburg is not in dispute. Besides the government saying it was only a "meteor," two different observatories stated they had tracked a "fireball" plunging toward Earth at a steep angle, as it passed over the Detroit area. So again, the fact "something" crashed near Kecksburg is simply not in dispute.

What is in dispute is why the government lied so massively about the number and types of military personnel it sent to Kecksburg in the immediate aftermath of the incident. These lies were in direct contradiction to statements by many local eyewitnesses and even the Greensburg *Tribune-Review*.

John Murphy, a journalist on site at the time was disturbed by the huge disparity between the government's later version and the version (again, amazingly consistent) by many of the witnesses at the time. According to his widow, he had been one of the first to reach the crash site and so saw the object.

Later, disturbed by the government's altered recounting of the events; he decided to investigate, planned on doing a radio documentary about the whole episode. As he approached the end of his investigation, he reported to friends he was onto something "big."

Then, John claimed two men in suits, apparently two MIBs (Men In Black) showed up suddenly and announced. They said something to John Murphy, which he never repeated to anyone else. However, they also told him that any future revealing of information about the Kecksburg Incident on his part would result in "severe consequences" for him, as he said they put it. They then confiscated all his evidence and documentation pertaining to his investigation. Moreover, they never informed him as to which branch of the government they supposedly represented. Who they actually were, remained a complete mystery to John.

However, whatever they said to Mr. Murphy, it seems to have scared him into silence. He did ultimately do a radio show, but it was nothing more than a simple recounting of the supposed "meteor" crash. No references to UFOs were included, none.

Depressed by the outcome of events, he went into an emotional nosedive and ended by losing his job shortly later. Once having been vociferous on the topic of the Kecksburg Incident, John no longer wished to discuss the matter with anyone in any way, or to any real extent.

Several years later, John Murphy seemed to feel it might be safe again to look into the matter of the crash at Kecksburg and told friends this fact. His fear of the MIBs seemed to have finally gone and he was in a much better state of mind, they said. Perhaps, after several years, he felt it was then safe to delve into the matter once more.

Two days later, a hit-and-run driver killed him while crossing a road. He was on a vacation at the time. Nobody ever found the driver who did this. It seems the minute word spread of John again having an interest in what happened that fateful night at Kecksburg; he had sealed his fate and assured his death. John Murphy suffered those "severe consequences," it would seem. John Murphy died in February of 1969, while on a trip to California.

Dr. James McDonald. June 13, 1971. Dr McDonald was senior physicist at the Institute of Atmospheric Physics. Furthermore, he was an acting professor at the University of Arizona, in the Department of Meteorology. Supposedly, he shot himself in the head.

Prior to this event, Dr. McDonald had worked tirelessly to motivate Congress into seriously looking into the issue of UFOs. Furthermore, he knew without a doubt, as he put it, that for those who wanted to maintain secrecy about the subject of UFOs he was getting to be a real problem. Despite this, throughout the 1960's, he steadfastly tried to pressure Congress into performing official investigations of the whole UFO matter.

Is this just another suddenly depressed scientist? It would seem there was more to the story than just this, since he didn't die of the gunshot wound. He was wheelchair bound. Despite this sad state of affairs for him, just a few months later, somehow, someway, and this seems to stretch one's credulity, he managed to get in his car. He drove to a pawnshop, managed to get out of his car and into the shop. There, he bought a gun, and then traveled all the way to a remote desert area where he shot himself, this time more successfully, since it resulted in his death this time.

Of course, considering the bizarre and extraordinary circumstances and lengths he had to go to do this, it does make wonder about the validity of his supposed suicide. Surely, there were easier means closer at hand for a paraplegic than to resort to such incredible efforts to do himself in? Why not just wheel himself out into the nearest busy road, for instance?

Philip K. Dick. Famous as a science fiction writer of the very strange and macabre, this author died in March of 1982. His books dealt very much with such things as dystopian societies and dangerous forms of government, as well as superpowerful corporations that could rule with iron fists, etc. Among his works were: *Bladerunner, A Scanner Darkly, The Man In The High Castle, Minority Report,* and many more. Obviously, a number of movies came about from some of these stories, so the author's reputation was a good one. He was high profile, well known…perhaps too well known as it turns out.

Mr. Dick suffered a stroke and later died under what many have referred to as "somewhat mysterious circumstances." It is said he had been writing a personal book, one on his firsthand experiences with extraterrestrials, his having had contact with them in some way, at least, purportedly. The book was never published and even the original manuscript, itself, seems to have vanished forever. Where did it go? This is just another unanswered question.

I include the author in this list because of the odd events surrounding his death, as well as the fact of what he'd been working on at the time of his death, interaction with aliens in some way. If he had been a less known, a less important author and one who few had heard of or read, I wouldn't have included him here.

However, because of his far-reaching fan base, anything he wrote would have hit the media. The media would have commented on his book and it would have been widely read. So was his death to stop his final book from being published and read? We may never know, but perhaps "someone" does. In any case, this was an intriguing enough case I felt it should be included here.

Captain Don Elkin, Pilot. Don Elkin's death was supposedly a suicide committed in 1984. Again, we have someone who was writing a book at the time of his demise. He had been suffering from a worsening illness, and this could have well been the reason for his suicide. However, the fact he was writing a book at the time of his death, as well, and just as Mr. Dick had, is curious and coincidental to say the least. Moreover, he was convinced there was a UFO conspiracy cover-up and had spent the prior ten years of his life exploring this issue. His death was hardly the end of such strange demises. In fact, the deaths just kept coming and even picked up in their frequency.

Avtar Singh-Guide, January 1987. This scientist and researcher simply disappeared. Much later, they pronounced him dead, although what happened to him remains a mystery to this day. He simply vanished, as had others before him.

Peter Pippel, February 1987. Peter was killed in an odd accident when he was hit by his car and in of all places, in his garage. A strange way to die, indeed, to say the least.

David Sands, March 1987. Reports say Mr. Sands died of a suicide attempt by deliberately running his vehicle into a building.

Shani Warren, April 1987. MS. Warren died in a so-called accidental drowning.

Mark Wiesner, April 1987. Mr. Wiesner supposedly committed suicide by hanging himself, although people, relatives and friends, have no idea why he would do such a thing.

David Greenhalgh, April 1987. He apparently just happened to fall off a bridge. This seems to have happened more than once as a way of such particular people dying. It would seem bridges aren't safe for researchers/scientists/investigators to cross. They seem to have a higher than normal accident rate while doing this. Somehow, they tend to topple over the railings, despite the railings being there to stop this very thing from happening.

Stuart Gooding, April 1987. Here I have yet another person who was murdered. Exactly why this happened is a matter for conjecture.

Michael Baker, May 1987. Mr. Baker died in a car accident.

The point here with this year, 1987, is just how many people died in so short of time. This is one of those "clusters of death" others have mentioned. Any of the deaths (except for some), might be construed as "just one of those things." However, the sheer number of them seems distinctly odd, too much so. Yet, again, it doesn't end here. Death, like life it seems, goes on.

Dan Casolaro, 1991. Investigative reporter, Dan Casolaro, purportedly died by an act of suicide in 1991. Again, we have yet another suicide. At the time of his death, he had been investigating something called Project Promise, which was software that someone had stolen. Allegedly, this software could be used as a means of tracking anyone, no matter where on Earth they might be. Moreover, Dan allegedly had been actively pursuing information about Area 51, Pine Gap, and more.

Why he would commit suicide when he seemed so intent, so deep into such investigations is curious, to say the very least. Moreover, this is yet one more in the number of apparent "suicides" with regard to those investigating UFOs. These kept mounting, to the point where it now begins to stretch one's credulity in the matter. The same holds true for murders, as well.

Ron Rummel. Again, we have yet another suicide, this time of a retired intelligence agent for the Air Force. He died August 6, 1993. Ron Rummel also had an active interest in UFOs, of course, which is why I mention him here. Once more, as with many other such deaths, there were mysterious circumstances surrounding it.

Mr. Rummel purportedly shot himself with a pistol. However, some of those who were on the scene shortly after his demise, claim there was no blood to be found on the gun, despite his having put the weapon in his mouth to commit his supposed suicide. Furthermore, there were no fingerprints on the gun. Moreover, there are those who now claim that although Mr. Rummel was right-handed, his suicide note was written by a left-handed person.

Mr. Rummel, before his demise, had published a magazine titled ***Alien Digest***. He had focused at times on the idea aliens might just be using humans as some sort of food source and/or for organ bank parts. This is, of course, a highly disturbing accusation; one usually relegated to pure science fiction, such as in the famous, even iconic episode of **Twilight Zone**, *To Serve Man*.

So we have to at least raise the question, if this was perhaps too close to some sort of truth, and therefore, he had to be silenced? In any case, this is one more suicide of someone intimately involved in the subject of UFOs at the time of his death. Likewise, nobody can understand why he would commit suicide. As one person put it, he hardly "seemed the type." The list goes on.

Ron Johnson. June 1994. Deputy Director of MUFON, Rob Johnson died under mysterious circumstances. Shortly before his death at age 43, he'd had a complete physical, which found nothing wrong, but rather to the contrary, found him to be in very good condition.

However, while attending a meeting in Austin, Texas, he collapsed and died in a matter of seconds. His face turned a deep shade of purple and blood came from his nose. This was just after sipping from a soft drink. His symptoms did not appear to be those of a stroke or anything "natural," although the authorities ascribed his death to such.

However, there were some peculiar things involved with Mr. Johnson before his demise. He is said to have attended two meetings at NATO, clandestine ones. He had been a part of a think tank before leaving there, and this supposedly involved his having security clearances, high ones at the time. Moreover, the symptoms of his death also could just as easily have been ascribed to poisoning. His generally great state of health, as well as his comparatively young age, again being just 43, also make his death an anomalous one.

So just of what did he actually die? Was it natural causes or murder? His official autopsy stated the cause of his death was "inconclusive." This, in itself, seems very strange under the circumstances. Why was it inconclusive? Surely, an autopsy would have revealed a brain hemorrhage, an aneurism, or any such type of thing.

Phil Schneider, January 17, 1996. The found Mr. Schneider strangled to death with a catheter tube around his throat. His life was as controversial as the manner of his death, perhaps even more so, for he claimed to have worked at secret government installations, one at Dulce, New Mexico, for example, where aliens were supposedly based/working with their human counterparts.

Among his many controversial declarations is there had been a "misunderstanding" with these "grays," a type of alien there, and an ensuing battle in which humans were killed, as well as some of the extraterrestrials. It was during this confrontation Mr. Schneider was supposedly wounded, burned in the chest by some laser or particle beam weapon of the aliens. This was later to cause him cancer, as he claimed. He did have the scars of a burn mark.

Mr. Schneider made a number of strange claims besides these, but one that concerns us here is that he swore attempts had been made to kill him before his actual death took place. He claimed he did not expect to survive for very long as a result.

He didn't. Some of his accusations about the government bordered on the bizarre, but there is evidence the CIA, as well as the FBI were actively "interested" in him. His wife said agents of those organizations entered and searched his home not long after his demise. She also said they confiscated a large number of "family" photographs.

Was Mr. Schneider murdered? Death by catheter, whether by accident or suicide, seems not only curious in the extreme, but highly unlikely, as well. As we all know, it's very hard to strangle one's self, and that's precisely why most people who choose this form of death hang themselves.

Ann Livingston, November 1994. An investigator for MUFON, MS. Livingston died in 1994. Not too long before her death, in November 1993, she had written an article for the MUFON Journal, *Electronic Harassment and Alien Abductions*. In this article, she spoke about the Director of the Electronic Surveillance Project for the Association of National Security Alumni, Julianne McKinney.

Apparently, McKinney dismissed the whole UFO question as just things the government was doing, either as some form of psychological testing on people, and/or testing of prototype equipment of various sorts. Ann Livingston's death came just months after this article went to print. Prior to her death in 1992, she claimed to have witnessed a bright light outside of her apartment. She also claimed she was later accosted by the so-called Men In Black, five of them.

She described them as "*being almost faceless.*" Furthermore, she states they had used some type of "*flashlight-like*" objects, which resulted in her becoming unconscious. As strange as this might sound, MS. Livingston swore all this to be true.

Later, her death came in the form ovarian cancer, a particularly fast-acting type of the disease. Various investigators have wondered just what caused this illness, if perhaps, the Men In Black and what they had done to her might have been the reason. As another side note, MS Livingston had also claimed to have experienced an alien abduction some time prior to all this.

Dr. Karla Turner. Here is another case along these lines. MS. Turner, an author, spoke publicly about the possibility and her fear of retribution (alien) for daring to voice her beliefs in her writings. She died in 1996 of breast cancer.

Was her death really of natural causes? Alternatively and as some claim, had someone induced her cancer, even as others claimed Ann Livingston's illness was? The subject is controversial, to say the least. However, it should be remembered that cancers can be induced in some cases, as in some rat trials, by injecting cancerous cells into healthy animals, so the idea isn't as farfetched as one might believe.

MS. Mae Bussell. Along these same lines, is the death of Mae Busell, who also died of a rapidly growing cancer. She, too, had an interest and involvement in the whole question of UFOs, and was an investigative radio journalist/host, as well.

More Deaths:

Jim and coral Lorenzen 1986—1988, respectively. Members and directors of an Arizona organization involved with the question of UFOs, APRO, they, each of them, died of cancer, and just a couple of years apart.

Astronaut Dick Slayton, 1993. He, too, died of cancer, and this was just before he was supposedly planning to divulge his own involvement with UFOs while being an astronaut. Dick Slayton was one of the original astronauts for NASA.

I can go on. A large number of researchers and scientists associated with the so-called Star Wars, or Strategic Defense Initiative promoted by then President Regan also died over a short time span. There were over thirty of these deaths and they include, but are not limited to:

Roger Hill, death by supposed suicide in 1985, **Jonathan Walsh**, who, like Secretary Forrestal, fell from his room at a hotel in 1985, and this after telling others he was concerned someone might kill him. There was also **Ashad Sharif**, who allegedly killed himself in a bizarre way, by wrapping a rope around his neck, securing it to a nearby tree, and then getting in his car and trying to drive away. **Peter Ferry,** apparently somehow killed himself and in an unusual way. They found him. He him, electrocuted by having had live wires placed inside his mouth. The question has to be raised, why not just hold onto them, instead, if suicide was his intent? This almost seems more like a form of torture, or perhaps an object lesson for others?

Apparently, **Alistair Beckham,** an engineer**,** did decide to use this method, as well, or so we are told. When they discovered him, purportedly he had electrocuted himself, too, but this time by having wires attached to his body. He went a step further, apparently, because there was a wadded up handkerchief in his mouth. If this was suicide, it beggars the imagination why he would do it in such a way. Why the handkerchief in his mouth? Was it to prevent him screaming? Would a man intent on killing himself care about that?

It doesn't stop there. **Trevor Knight** died in his automobile, asphyxiated by carbon monoxide. Was this a suicide, as well? Nobody seems sure. **Andrew Hall** also died in a similar manner, by carbon monoxide.

The reason these deaths are UFO related is that President Regan, and on more than one occasion, talked about the threat of an alien invasion, including in a speech at the UN. Furthermore, questions have been raised as to the whole purpose of the SDI program, its real *raison d'être*, or reason for being.

Some conspiracy theorists even say the program had ties to aliens, who were involved in helping with the program. These conspiracy theorists claim those who discovered this truth, were then "dealt with." Others say the real purpose of SDI was as a protection against extraterrestrials, and this reason had to stay hidden. Additionally, they say when the program ended, certain researchers and scientists couldn't be trusted to keep quiet so they "had to go."

As I close on this period of deaths of such scientists, researchers, journalists, and UFO investigators, there is one more thing I should mention and that is Sydney Sheldon's List.

Sidney Sheldon's List. Sydney Sheldon, the world-famous author of mysteries and thrillers, etc., when writing his recent book, *End Of The World*, had compiled a real-life list of scientists and researchers who had all died over a very short period of time and under mysterious circumstances. No less than 25 such persons in this category met their untimely demise in this period. Mr. Sheldon first noticed this phenomenon and although his book is one of fiction, he truly felt the deaths of the real people were related to the whole question of there being real aliens, as well.

Rash of Deaths in Early 2000s. Here we have another "cluster" of deaths of scientists, researchers, UFO investigators, and authors engaged in writing such topics.

William Milton Cooper, November 2001. Author of the now popular and famous book, *Behold A Pale Horse* (1991), he was shot dead by police after acting very strangely and supposedly resisting arrest. He had been an avid UFO researcher and investigator, and felt sure the government was "*out to get him*," a remark he made a number of times to friends and associates.

That he suffered from delusions toward the end of his life is without doubt. However, the circumstances of his death, being so self-prophetic, are curious, if not outright disturbing. The police shot him in his home.

However, the police had arranged for medical help to be standing by when they stormed his home. They did this in advance of their assault. Whether this was for themselves, for him, or both, is uncertain. What is certain is the police seemed to "expect" bloodshed, whereas in many other similar cases, there are no trauma/ambulances called in advance to similar such scenes. So why in this case alone?

Deaths of Microbiologists. Then there are the deaths of microbiologists and not just any microbiologists, but often world-renowned ones. These occurred in a cluster and their deaths occurred over a wide geographic area. The closeness in time of these deaths makes them suspicious in nature, as well, not to mention some of the circumstances.

Dean Stonier, August 2001. Intimately involved in the Global Sciences Congress, Dean was the victim of a sudden fatal heart attack.

Benito Que. November 2001. Brutally attacked and ultimately dying from a beating, this was while he was in Miami.

Don C. Wiley, November 2001. They found his body in a river in Memphis, Tennessee. Detectives claim that he became "dizzy" and so met his death by accident, falling from a bridge into the river. Again, where were those protective railings and why hadn't they stopped his fall?

Vladimir Pasechnik, November 2001. He died as the result of a massive stroke.

Robert Schwartz, December 2001. Again, another case of death by attack. He was viciously stabbed to death in Leesburg, Virginia. As a curious side note, it was three supposed Satanists who the police arrested and charged with the crime.

Nguyen Van Set, December 2001. This is a strange sort of death. Nguyen perished while in an airlock. He died of nitrogen asphyxiation. This took place in Geelong, at the very southern tip of the east coast of Australia.

Victor Korshunov February 2002. Assaulted and bludgeoned to death in Moscow, Russia, he died very close to his home.

Ian Langford, February 2002. This death was particularly bizarre. They found his body shoved under a chair and in a partial state of undress. This happened in Norwich, the United Kingdom.

Tanya Holzmayer, February 2002. Murdered by a fellow microbiologist, the murderer then committed suicide.

David Wynn-Williams, March 2002. He died in a highway collision near Cambridge, the United Kingdom.

Steven Mostow, March 2002. Steven died in plane crash, a plane he, himself, was piloting at the time near Denver, Colorado. He was involved with the Colorado Health Sciences Center.

Paul Vegay, February 2009. Paul Vegay was a leading expert on crop circles. So familiar was he with the subject and so well known for this fact, Mel Gibson turned to him to help him work on his movie, **Signs**. The result was a movie that was both frightening and accurate in most respects.

Mr. Vegay met an untimely death not long after the movie was made. How he died is a mystery. Nobody seems to know, nor does there seem to be a great deal of interest in finding out, at least not by the police and/or other authorities. His body was found floating in the sea near Portsmouth, England. The actual cause of this death is uncertain. How did he end up there? That's the question UFO researchers want answered.

Conclusion. So it goes and continues to go. Death after death, some appearing to be of natural causes, but the sheer number of those making them suspect. Moreover, despite the number of deaths we've listed here, these are but a portion of the total.

What can we take from all these many deaths, some of which seem very peculiar in nature? Well, we know they seemed to have started shortly after the Roswell Incident, which took place in 1947. The first significant death seems to have taken place in 1949 with Secretary Forrestal.

From there, the number and frequency of deaths accelerated. This in itself strongly suggests a tie-in with the whole UFO phenomenon, because all these people were in some way related to this in their work. Either that, or they were scientists who worked on clandestine projects that may have involved contact with extraterrestrials, or were designed to protect us from them, perhaps.

Now, we just can't know for sure. Their work in most cases has never been revealed to the public, so it's hard to say. All we have are inferences as to the nature of their work in some cases, but one thing we do know; many were involved in some way with the SDI program, for instance. The exact details of which, are still a mystery, however.

We have to take into account just who is dying and how they are dying. The statistically abnormally high number of deaths by heart attack and cancers in this group must be considered as suspect, as well. The occupations of all these people, being journalists, investigators, researchers, scientists, or even MUFON investigators, also would seem suspicious and we must factor this in, as well. Why so many of this particular group?

Then there are the "clusters" of deaths, as in 1987—1989, as well as in 2001—2002. Researchers claim the number of deaths skyrocketed in certain periods, times which coincided with the completion and/or cessation of certain black projects. This, too, seems curious

Furthermore, some of the bizarre types of supposed suicides and the questions still swirling around them also lend credence to concerns about this being part of a conspiracy of silence to shut those up who "someone" feels may be loose cannons, or were better "removed" once their work was done.

Finally, there are the blatant murders, such as John Murphy's death by a hit-and-run driver. Nobody ever caught the murderer and this happening just after he had decided to go ahead once more with his investigation of the Kecksburg Incident and only after having been warned of the repercussions by those mysterious government agents if he did so. The stabbing and beating to death of others, the "falling off" of bridges, all seem rather unlikely endings for so many of these people. It must give one pause as to how and why this is happening. We would be foolish not to at least question this.

One thing seems certain; the business of UFO investigations and/or related occupations seems to be risky, and sometimes to have fatal consequences. This must be of concern to any future potential investigators, make them leery of doing such a thing.

Perhaps, this is precisely what is wanted and these are object lessons by death as a warning to others who dare open doors they aren't supposed to, who probe too far into where they aren't wanted. There does seem to be credible evidence to support this contention as witnessed by the number of deaths listed above. However, do please remember these aren't all the deaths, but rather just a good representative sampling.

Author Timothy Hood theorized many of these deaths might have been due to the actions of "special forces," government ordered ones. If this is so, the whole affair takes on a new and dangerous connotation. It should be stressed here that Mr. Hood didn't believe it was people who "chased" UFOs who were targeted, so much as it was researchers, investigators, journalists, and scientists who might have been becoming too great an annoyance, or perhaps too close to getting to some truth the government didn't want revealed.

Other Ufologists take the extreme point of view that somehow extraterrestrials are involved in all this, may have had a direct "hand" in the killing of some of these people. Is this true?

At present, I have no way of knowing, but one thing does seem clear: there are quite a number of investigators into all this, past and present, who do feel that "something" is going on with all this, and that all these deaths are not just accidents or "natural." Some could well be natural, of course. Others are just downright suspicious!

Although I reserve judgment about the idea of extraterrestrial creatures being directly involved in such deaths, I do think that perhaps there might have been, and still might be, an ongoing targeting of such people by someone. The number of suicides, bizarre ones, the number of eerie murders, and those accidents, again such as falling off bridges or being crushed by "accident" in their own garages and by their own car, just seem too many and too much to be explained otherwise. Again, could some of them have been the result of normal types of deaths? Yes, certainly, and it would be likely. Still, it would certainly stretch the Laws of Probability if they all were.

CHAPTER 10—GIGANTIC UFOS?

"I am completely convinced that UFOs have an out-of-world basis."
—**Dr. Walther Riedel**

When I think of all the vanished aircraft, boats, and ships, this doesn't seem to be quite so far-fetched an idea, the concept of there being gigantic UFOs in our skies. They would explain what is happening to all the aircraft that disappear without a trace, and even smaller boats, and perhaps larger ones, as well. Otherwise, where have all these craft vanished to without a trace? Yes, undoubtedly some may have just sunk or crashed into the ocean, but how do we account for ones that just simply seem to vanish altogether?

Why do we never find any debris of so many aircraft, such as Valentich's, the bomber flying over the Mediterranean that disappeared, and even Moncla's jet, as well as so many others? It's as if they were swallowed completely by something. That something might just be UFOs. Then, they would have to be very large to do this. Do we have evidence for this, huge sizes of UFOs? Yes, in fact, we do.

First, do remember, too, that already some UFOs sighted are said to be massive. Even now, currently, people are spotting UFOs estimated to be 10 football fields in length. Other sightings have recorded objects so large, some have said they were a mile in diameter, as in the case of one UFO over the English Channel. This monster was much larger than any existing aircraft carrier. Moreover, the UFO had been seen by no less than two different aircraft and not only the navigational crews saw it, but so did passengers.

Japan Air Lines flight 1628, November 1986. In a much-heralded case at the time, and now considered a classic UFO sighting, this was a strange event, indeed. While flying over Alaska, near mount McKinley, the entire crew of flight 1628 saw two UFOs. They describe them as being walnut-shaped. The things buzzed and harassed the jet.

Eventually, the two of the UFOs flew off at high speeds and disappeared. However, a third and much larger UFO then came into view. So worried was the crew of the jet, they requested an alteration in their flight path to avoid the thing. This they received from the flight control tower.

Even so, the UFO continued to come too close to the jet, coming so close at times, the crew claimed they could feel the heat of the object through the windshield. The length of the sighting was just short of an hour in duration, a long time! The size of the object, according to the crew was huge and the dwarfed their jet in size.

Giant UFO, Paris, France, January 1994. Pilot Jean-Charles Doboc saw a large UFO near Paris. The object appeared to be at about 35,000 feet. Moreover, he estimated it was 800 feet in diameter or 2,513 feet in circumference. This is close to half a mile in circumference! The pilot reported the object to the Reims air-traffic control. He claimed the object was stationary or moving very slowly. Then he claimed the object faded from view even as he watched it, as if it had some sort of cloaking device, or as he put it "invisibility capability. He claimed to have seen the UFO clearly for almost a minute. Then, over a period of 10 to 20 seconds, it just faded slowly out of existence.

English Channel, June 2007. As reported by The Daily Mail, as well as other papers in Britain, a massive UFO was spotted over the English Channel. This all began in June 2007. A Trislander plane, piloted by Captain Ray Bowyer of the Aurigny Air Services was flying over the English Channel when he saw something strange. Being a clear day, he knew what he saw wasn't the result of some sort of weather anomaly.

What it was, he wasn't sure. There was a low layer of haze blocking any view of the ground, but at the altitude his plane was flying, 4000 feet, it was perfectly clear. Being so far away, he decided to use his binoculars. Through them, Captain Bowyer could see a large object, what he initially thought was about the size of a 737 Boeing jet. The thing was "cigar-shaped." It had a dark line bisecting the middle of it. He figured the thing was hovering just 2000 feet above ground level. Then he saw what he was sure was another object near the first.

Fifty years old and an experienced pilot, Captain Bowyer didn't know what to make of what he was seeing. He did not recognize the shape of the craft, it being inconsistent with anything he had ever seen before. Concerned, he radioed the Jersey Island control tower. He asked them if they could see an object on their radar.

The Captain knew a direct sighting of the objects from the ground might have been blocked by the haze below, but he felt they should show on radar even so. The radar tower responded in the negative. They had nothing on their screens. He countered, by requesting they check further. Minutes later, they radioed back they were picking up something, two "somethings" over the water near Alderny Island.

As he approached his destination, the pilot could see the UFO better. Now the object was clearly visible without the aid of binoculars. Nor was he alone in seeing the UFO. Being a small plane, there was no barrier between the pilot and his passengers. He could clearly hear their conversations as they talked about the UFOs. One thing was new; the dark line around the center of the craft had now resolved into a series of blue and green lights.

As he began to descend to land on Alderney Island, the UFOs disappeared in the haze. That was the end of their view of the strange craft. Nor was he alone in the sighting. Another plane, as well, had seen the object, or at least one of them. The plane was flying to Jersey, the Isle of Man. Listing on the radio, the pilot knew the control tower had seen something on their radar. Worried it might be a problem for him, as well, he scanned the skies to see if he could see what they were talking about.

Captain Patrick Patterson did see something. Dutifully, he reported it. He said he saw a cigar-shaped object. He further stated it was yellowish in color. Two passengers on the other plane had stated the UFO was an orange color, a very close description to that of Captain Patterson. However, due to the intervening haze, he only had sighted one of the objects for about a minute, or so.

Under British law, pilots are encouraged to report any sightings of an unusual nature, unlike here in the United States. This, Captain Bowyer did do, as well. After some further and careful consideration, he decided the object had to been much larger than he originally thought, to be seen so clearly from so far away. He estimated the object to be about a mile across.

So what did the UK government do about this? They had reliable reports from pilots of two different airplanes, as well as witnesses in the form of passengers on one of the planes. Yet, their response was peculiar.

First, they questioned the reliability of the radar tracking. Since the control tower had reported the object as being stationary, they decided since aircraft couldn't do this maneuver very well, not ones of such size, that something must have been wrong with the radar temporarily malfunctioning. As for the pilots' testimony, they seem to have disregarded that altogether. The summation of the report said, basically, since the objects were not in British airspace, they were really of no importance.

Really? Really? The UFOs may not have been exactly in British airspace, but they were very close to it, indeed. In any case, the sighting of a mile-wide object hovering over the English Channel should have been of concern to the United Kingdom government. Probably, in fact, it was. However, publicly, they were not concerned, or so they stated. This seems far too similar to many cases in the United States, how our government responds to them.

Huge Object Seen Over Chile, March 2014. Nor was the English Channel sighting the only sighting of something very large. On March 18, near the El Yeso Reservoir, a large UFO was seen. Witnesses described it as being twice the size of Chile's National Stadium. Photographs were taken. The *Comité de Estudios de Fenómenos Aéreos Anomalos*, or as it is better known, CEFFA, analyzed the photos and found them to be genuine, and not hoaxes. People had seen a giant UFO, according to them.

San Antonio, April 2014. Again, we have another reported, or actually several reports, of a huge object flying in our skies, one far too big to be aircraft known to any experts. This UFO was boomerang in shape. It traveled without making any noise. Additionally, this wasn't the first such incident of people seeing such a strange-shaped object in the skies over Texas. Numerous reports had been flooding in for some time. The size of these objects varied slightly, with some saying, they were the size of a Boeing 747 jet, but others saying they were as large as a football field.

Paris, France, November 2014. Another massive craft was sighted over Paris in November of 2014. As one witness described it:

"I caught a spectacular large craft over the Business center "La Défense", near Paris. The object was slowly moving between some buildings. It was right in the middle of my field of view, when I started recording with my iPhone."

The witness has the video to prove it.

Another witness stated:

"The object looked metallic, due to huge sun reflection on its side. It was clearly saucer-shaped, no doubt on this, you can't deny it."

Many other witnesses saw it as well, and they have their photos and videos to verify it actually happened. If one looks at the photos/video, one can't help but notice how huge the thing really is.

So what are we to make of all this? We don't just have UFOs in our skies, but sometimes have truly massive ones, and these have been reported for decades. Giant, silent, massive UFOs drift through our skies without compunction. We seem powerless to stop and/or interfere with them.

Likewise, despite videos, photographs and endless testimony by reliable witnesses, such as airplane pilots, navigators, etc., no government around the world seems to be taking this very seriously. At least they don't, not publicly. Despite constant violations of national airspace, the governments around the world not only do nothing, but they seem to say very little, as well. One has to ask, just why this is? Why are they so dismissive, again, at least in public?

Moreover, there seems to be evidence that these things can hide themselves. The term *"made itself invisible,"* has been used more than once. They seem to appear and then disappear, and sometimes, this happens in front of multiple witnesses.

What does this mean? Well, if they have some sort of cloaking device, such as seen on the fictional television program, **Star Trek**, then they may be in our skies far more often than we realize and we just can't see them. In other words, they could be hovering overhead at any time, and unless for some reason wished to make themselves visible, we just wouldn't know.

If this sounds farfetched, think about our own stealth fighters and bombers, that although being large aircraft, they have the radar signature of a normal bird. Furthermore, we are even now experimenting seriously with our own invisibility/cloaking devices, as well. Just how far the government might have gotten in this endeavor, is of course, not known to the public. It would naturally be a closely guarded secret.

So perhaps we just can't determine the presence of extraterrestrial craft in our skies if they don't want us to do so, at least, perhaps not in daytime. Or can we? Might we have some technological means to discern their existence, even when we can't see them with our naked eyes? Possibly, this might be so, because there is the example of this having happened, too. A

Japanese civilian while taking photographs of planes taking off at an airport didn't see anything out of the ordinary, or unusual. However, when he later looked at the photographs, there was the distinct image of a UFO there. He had seen nothing when looking himself, and he had been looking carefully, sighting to take his pictures. Nevertheless, although he couldn't see it, the camera had captured the image of a UFO.

So how do these truly gigantic UFO's relate to the idea of disappeared planes, and/or boats? Well, it seems there are UFOs quite capable of literally engulfing such craft, swallowing them up, and perhaps this is what happened with Lieutenant Moncla back in the 1950s.

Remember, he, Lieutenant Wilson, and their jet disappeared, seemingly forever. As a further instance of this, the movie, **Close Encounters of the Third Kind**, did have several pilots returned, disgorged from a massive "mothership." Yes, this movie was fiction, but the idea for this had to come from somewhere. Additionally, given the size of UFOs reported during the time, the movie was made, and since then and on such a regular basis, perhaps the idea isn't quite as fictional as one might first have thought.

Do UFOs abduct entire planes and perhaps some boats, as well? One can't say for sure, but judging by the size of some of the UFOs that have been witnessed, it could be a distinct possibility. They certainly seem big enough.

PART 3—THE TRULY BIZARRE

"We must stop asking: Can these things be? And begin asking: Why are these things?"
—**John Keel**

CHAPTER 11—DEADLY FORBIDDEN ZONES?

"In my mind, there is no question that they're out there."
—**Professor Michio Kaku**

Vile Vortices, the Deadly Triangles. We won't spend a great deal of time on this topic, since most of us have already heard, read, and seen much on TV about it all. For instance, for decades now, people have been talking about the Bermuda Triangle. Few people in the United States aren't aware of this strange region. To a lesser extent, but still prominent, is the so-called Dragon's Triangle in Southeast Asia. In fact, more ships and planes have been lost in this area than in the Bermuda Triangle.

However, these aren't the only places in the world where this sort of strange phenomenon seems to be going on. According to Ivan Sanderson, there are twelve such areas and they can exist on land, as well as in our seas. Some regions of the Earth seem almost to be forbidden zones, ones forbidden to us humans, at least, because death and disappearances result.

This is so with the Bermuda Triangle and the Dragon's Triangle, but it also is true of such places as Mexico's Zone of Silence. Having traveled through the region, I can personally vouch for many of its odd characteristics. These include, according to those who have researched it, strange deformed plants in the region, some animal mutations, as well as a weird blanketing effect on varying forms of radio communication.

There is no doubt for me about this last one. I had significant problems with my own radio equipment in this area. Devices that worked fine before entering it, became terribly unreliable or just didn't seem to function at all within the region. Upon leaving the area, they again worked. Even planes flying at good altitudes have experienced this phenomenon, as well.

Other things malfunctioned. A test firing of an American missile strayed incredibly far off course to crash into this zone, when it shouldn't have done so. UFO sightings are common there, as well. There is even a site of a supposed crashed UFO. There is evidence something might have done this still there, in the form of marks and damage to the area, although the Mexican government (with the aid of the US military, some insist) removed any materials and remains of such a craft from the area. Meteorites seem "drawn" to the region, as one researcher put it, as if there was some sort of attractive force there for them.

Another vile vortex is located in the Sahara desert. This one is even more sinister in some respects. This is because animal life, according to the scientist, Dr. Joseph Spencer, has a hard time thriving there, or doesn't survive at all. Furthermore, he claims animals forced to go into the area begin to go insane after a while. He has a rather valid case for this, firsthand knowledge of a terrible sort.

He had taken his son and the family dog along with him for a short day trip into the area. After a time, the dog began to become agitated, nervous, and was unable to settle down. This worsened. Taking a short break, Dr. Spencer stopped the car to do a little exploring close by the vehicle, within sight of it, but a couple of hundred yards away from it. This way, he could keep the car and so his son in sight.

What he didn't know was that the dog had become violent. It attacked his son inside the car and killed him. Returning to the scene, the distraught Dr. Spencer swung open the door only to be confronted by the sight of his son bleeding to death. The dog rushed past him and out of the vehicle. The animal took off across the desert and was never seen again. This had always been a perfectly gentle and loving family pet prior to this episode. The dog had never been any trouble whatsoever the entire time they had owned it.

This heartbreaking and tragic event caused Dr. Spencer to begin investigating the area. He discovered the region had long been known as a strange place, with animals and even insects seeming to shun it, and with people disappearing on an ongoing basis. The place is known as "the Devil's Graveyard," and perhaps with good reason. Poor Dr. Spencer and his son found this out firsthand.

An odd thing about these 12 "Vile Vortices," as that when on land, they have megaliths in these areas, or very close by. Alternatively, something very strange happened there or continues to happen. For instance, the ruins of Mohenjo-Daro lie in one of these vortices. This ancient city has undergone something very peculiar. Archaeologists have found in the lower layers of the ruins evidence of a fire of great intensity.

There is an area, circular in nature, where on one side, the stonework facing toward the center of this roughly circular region, has been vitrified. Only volcanoes (volcanic activity of some sort), or thermonuclear weapons could produce such intense heat, with the exception of a possible asteroid impact. However, there is no evidence for any asteroid impact happening in Mohenjo-Daro, and there is no volcanic activity of any sort in the area, either. This leaves only the possibility of the event having been nuclear in nature.

Once again, ordinary fires, any of those produced by man or nature simply don't get nearly hot enough to turn stone and rock into glass, which once more, is the definition of vitrification for our purposes here. Heat of such intensity wasn't even available to us until very recent times. Did a nuclear blast occur in Mohenjo-Daro? Something strange certainly did.

The 12 "Vile Vortices are, in alphabetical order: Algerian Megaliths (Devil's Graveyard), Bermuda Triangle, Devil's Sea or Dragon's Triangle, Easter Island, Hamakulia, Mohenjo-Daro, New Hebrides Trench, North Pole, South Atlantic Anomaly, South Pole, Wharton Basin, and the Zimbabwe Megaliths. These are evenly spaced out, above and below the equator and they encircle the Earth.

Some of these areas have much better documentation regarding strange events occurring there than others. This is because some are located nearer to heavily populated places than others. Nevertheless, all these inexplicable regions have one thing in common; that is, people vanish without a trace, as do planes, boats, and ships.

People see UFOs more often in such regions, more than in other locales north or south of such areas. In fact, there seems a distinct association or correlation of UFO sightings along the latitudes of these "vile vortices," and much more so than in other areas. This phenomenon is reported to be true right around the world.

What are these places, these vile vortices? The theories are many. Some say they are weak points in space/time, and so are doorways to other dimensions or alternate realities. Others say they are power points on the Earth, where some unknown form of energy emits (thus causing all the problems for people and animals who try to inhabit the regions).

Adherents of this theory say UFOs use this energy either as a power source or as a sort of navigational grid system, as ley lines are said to be. Some even say they are doorways for UFOs to enter and exit our world through some type of star gates and/or wormholes. As to the point of origin of such beings, this is open to conjecture. Some say they come from other star systems and others say other universes entirely. Although I don't discount these ideas, I would need to see more evidence for this before agreeing that such hypotheses/theories are true. As it stands, for me at least, the evidence is still rather meager.

However, it could be possible, because there is evidence ley lines do exist. In Europe, major ancient megalithic structures do seem to follow these lines across the continent very well. They form perfect lines as the crow flies.

There are other signs of these ley lines, as well. In Southern Europe, for example, whether France or Italy, all along one ley line there are town and villages. This, in itself, is common. Europe's a highly populated place and there are villages and towns everywhere. However, the fact the towns along this ley line have names that derive from the root word "star" from their area's ancient languages is extremely weird. Why would this be? Why would the oldest population centers, whether villages or towns, all have names with the root word "star" in them and over such a long line, such a vast distance?

There is something else with regard to the idea of forbidden zones. As mentioned earlier in this book, with regard to the Dyatlov Pass Incident in Russia, the local tribes' people had names for such regions as the "Mountain of the Dead," and literally, "Don't Go There." This clearly demonstrates people, their people, had been warned in an official way. These names were akin to our signs, signs such as "Forbidden Entry," "Hazardous Material," "Biohazard," etc. In short, they were formalized warnings to stay away from those places. They were "forbidden."

This Russian region isn't the only place with such warnings attached to it for centuries. In addition, there is a place farther west in Russia, in the Siberian region that has the same sort of strange names, but about something else entirely.

This "something" involves, of all things, the so-called "cauldrons." For centuries, it seems there have been rumors in this area of large metal caldrons, or half-domes. There are circular indentations in swamps where some were said to have been once, but have since sunk into the marsh. There is the tale of one traveler who told of sleeping inside one of the cauldrons for shelter against the cold with some friends (they are very big cauldrons, it seems), and then later suffering ill effects. The symptoms were similar to radiation sickness.

He didn't die, but others did. He did become ill to some degree, suffered various health problems thereafter, and had strange growths occur, but only on the side of his body where he lay in the cauldron against the metal. Rumors swirl these strange things may be radioactive, as a result.

Again, these so-called cauldrons have been there a long time. So long, in fact has this been, the locals named some regional features for them, such as the Cauldron River or Stream. The name of the area, literally, is the Valley of Death in the native tongue of the people there.

The cauldrons have various names in the local tongues, as well, one being Kheldyu, which literally translates into English as "iron house." Again, these are large structures. They apparently house metal rooms or chambers within them and one was purported to have had even a sort of metal spiral staircase in it. They allegedly resemble hemispheres with smooth surfaces, made of some copper or perhaps copper/bronze alloy. Whatever the metal is, it's extremely hard and resistant to damage. Hammers slammed against it bounce off harmlessly.

What is their purpose and from where did these things come? Well, theories abound, but one of the main ones is they were placed there centuries ago by extraterrestrials, since it seems highly doubtful humans of the time could build such uncharacteristically large objects all of metal. As to their purpose, they do seem to have a correlation to meteor strikes. The whole region seems to have a history of such meteor strikes that is higher in frequency than the worldwide average. This even includes the Tunguska Blast of 1908.

Some theorize the structures were a sort of space defense system for the region. They claim they were to shoot down incoming objects, such as whatever caused the Tunguska Blast, as well as other objects, such as meteors. These act as targets for these things. Some say they still function, or did until recently. Some researchers into the subject even contemplate the cauldrons act to draw such things to them, and again point to the unusually high incidence of meteorite impacts in the regions throughout the last few centuries.

So, is this another forbidden zone? If not the region, the cauldrons themselves definitely would seem to be. Ancient warnings abound about approaching them too closely. Their mysterious nature has also been a topic of conversation for a long time by the locals, centuries, and not in a good way. Stories of illnesses and deaths caused by the cauldrons are common.

Again, so long have these things been a supposed feature of the landscape, they have become an integral part of the people's history. To top it all off, strange moving lights in the sky are a common feature of the places where the cauldrons are supposed to be. Again, we have that strong connection to UFOs.

Whatever the vile vortices or these forbidden zones really are, whatever their cause, they are strange places, indeed. They can also be unusually deadly places, as well, it seems. Unless one has a very good reason to go there, one might wish to exercise some caution about such a decision. Additionally, their connection to UFOs, strange lights in the sky, etc., is a long and well-established one.

Finally, one can't say much good about these vile vortices, or forbidden zones. The very names of them are indicative of the fact they are seen as dangerous. So here, we have yet another correlation to UFOs and it is most definitely not a positive one, but rather just the opposite. In the vile vortices, where UFOs are often seen, people vanish, become ill, and die. As we can see at this point, this seems to be a common thread, a strong linkage to the idea UFOs can be and are dangerous to us humans. Still there is more…

CHAPTER 12—ABDUCTIONS

"Of course it is possible that UFO's really do contain aliens as many people believe, and the Government is hushing it up."
—**Professor Stephen Hawking**

The subject of abductions takes up much space in countless books on UFOs. Therefore, I do not intend to belabor the subject here. That abductions have been going on for a long time is obvious to anyone who has ever read any books on the phenomenon of UFOs. However, some might not be aware of just how far back in time this goes. Many think it sort of all began with Betty and Barney Hill in the early Sixties. It didn't. The occurrences go back much further than that!

The idea of the abductions of people by extraterrestrials in UFOs, and then returned to Earth, goes back millennia. From ancient times to now, accounts of people disappearing, sometimes for long periods, and then returning without knowing where they had been, proliferate throughout historical literature from cultures around the world.

Whether it is prophets of the Old Testament, such as Elijah, Enoch, or Moses ascending into our skies, the Prophet Mohammad taken up from the Dome of the Rock in Jerusalem, humans have supposedly risen from the Earth without first having had to die. In addition, many of them have been returned. Even Jesus Christ, as with him saying in the Bible in John 3:13:

"And no man hath ascended up to heaven, but he that came down from heaven, even the Son of man which is in heaven."

Nor are these references just confined to the Bible, whether Old Testament or New. Other cultures have a long and rich tradition of beings superior to themselves, taking people from Earth. For example, the gods from Mount Olympus scooped up innocent Greeks and seemingly carried them off whenever they felt like it. For the Chinese, fire-breathing dragons (alien spaceships?) did the same job. The Hopi people of the American Southwest have similar tales of interactions with "sky" or "star people."

Therefore, there are numerous stories throughout various cultures and at different times through history of people being the objects of abductions. Of course, they didn't think of these as being by extraterrestrials. Their idea of the identity of abductors was that they were demons, gods, angels, God, the Devil, "sky people," "sky guardians," or what have you.

Then, such ancient societies didn't have (in many cases) a concept of outer space or life on planets around other stars. Nevertheless, there were some notable exceptions to this, as with the Indian Vedic texts, which seem quite knowledgeable about such things, too knowledgeable for the times, many feel.

There is another curious phenomenon, too, and this is the idea of the "changeling." Throughout history, and again in various cultures around the world, there have been stories of abducted babies or children. These tales say that sometimes "replacements" are left behind as substitutes. Moreover, these replacements may look exactly like the original child, but they aren't.

Rather, they are a changeling, a duplicate of sorts. In such tales, often the child looks the same, but behaves very differently; often this is in evil ways. There have been various accusations as to who is at fault for these abductions, again including the devil, demons, and even, sadly, "Travelers," once called "Gypsies." Anyone who is different, anyone who is new to any area, often took the blame for such occurrences. Even when I was growing up, I was warned that if I didn't behave, "the gypsies would carry me off." Actually, at times, this seemed like a good idea to me. It beat cleaning out the garage as I had been ordered to do on one occasion, or so I felt at the time.

Now, at this point, I could cite endless cases of abductions. I will not do this. Again, this is for the reason you can look them up on the Internet, or find lengthy and detailed recitals of such cases in any of a hundred or more books on UFOs. There are whole books devoted just to listing such abduction cases and to giving the details of them. To repeat them here would then be pointless.

Please note, however, that many ufologists believe the number of abductions now number over a million, or perhaps even in the millions. If even a fraction of these is true, say, just 10%, we're still talking about hundreds of thousands of abductions worldwide. The abduction phenomenon also seems to take place all over our planet. Nowhere seems off limits to such extraterrestrial kidnappings of humans.

Are they really happening? I believe they are. The only alternative to this idea is all these people are the subject of some psychological problem, delusion, or hallucinations, which make them then think these abductions really happened to them. Of course, some of that might well be true, but all of them? I doubt if even a good fraction of those who say they have been abducted are lying, or the victims of some sort of delusion.

As a MUFON Field Investigator and a long-time researcher of the phenomenon prior to that position, I've met many people who I not only considered sane and intelligent, but even more so than the average person. When they relate an abduction case to me, I listen carefully looking for flaws. Most times, I find none. Moreover, I'm thoroughly convinced most of these people are telling the truth as they see it, at the very least.

What is the upshot of all this? Well, anyone who has read any books on the subject of abductions has to conclude that many of the people who claim such occurrences, or realize they have been abducted using hypnosis later on, are sane and responsible people. Remember, most have nothing to gain by claiming such a thing, except, perhaps, a very short-lived notoriety, which would place them in the limelight, and then being subjected to immense ridicule. Ridiculed by some, they often are, in fact, in most cases.

Therefore, just as with UFO sightings, people are very reluctant to come forth and talk about abductions for this very reason. In other words, I have to believe the majority of those who do come forth do so because they are brave individuals and they feel the need to share the experience, as well as to warn us.

There is one thing I should note about such abductions, as well. Unlike those who are permanently disappeared, which I will talk about later in this book, abductees are returned. They claim they are often the subject of terrible experimentation, or some type of medical procedures. Yet, ultimately, they come back to us.

So the question must arise, why are some returned while others, the permanently disappeared, are not? I feel this is an intriguing and important question, perhaps even a crucial one for us. However, what might be the reasons for this situation, the "returned" versus the "not returned?"

Well, there could be any number of reasons. However, there are some more likely answers than others in this case. They are:

1. Extraterrestrials are just performing experimentation or exploratory examinations on these abducted people, possibly implanting tracking devices, and then returning them, so they can continue to track their subjects. This is as we electronically might tag a wild animal under the same conditions. This would just be for research purposes and nothing else.

2. Extraterrestrials are taking people and performing some kind of operation, or procedure upon them to alter them in some way. In this case, the implants that have been found in some of the victims, or abductees (one can't help but think of them as being victims, though) may serve some other purpose other than just to track the abductee. This might mean that the individual has been genetically altered in some way, and the implant is to aid in this continuing effort.

Some UFO conspiracy theorists believe the human race may be in the process of being altered, and that a new, hybrid race that looks like us, but is not us, might already be in existence. If so, even the individuals involved may not be aware of this.

3. The third idea, and one I partially helped to come up with, is that extraterrestrials may be returning the abductees to us because they are now "sleepers." Just as during the Cold War that existed between the West and the Soviet Union for decades had their spies, and even "sleepers," (those were meant to go about their lives as if nothing was out of the ordinary until they were called upon to perform some predetermined action), perhaps extraterrestrials are doing the same.

This last is a frightening thought. With the number of returned abductees being at least one million and possibly quite a bit more, if they did turn out to be sleepers, we could be in real trouble. The premise for this is the idea such individuals aren't even aware they are sleepers. They wouldn't know a thing until the time came when they were "switched on."

The implants may be a form of programming that alters the brain functions of such abductees in such a way that they aren't consciously aware of it. However, perhaps under a given set of circumstances or conditions, something might trigger them to perform a certain way. In short, they might be programmed to aid extraterrestrials.

Why would an alien species do this? Well, as just an example, if they intended a future invasion of our world, it might help to have millions of programmed agents, ones we aren't even aware of, planted amidst the populations of our world. Just when we might be at the worse disadvantage, sleepers might "turn on," might suddenly appear on the scene to add to the general confusion, to misdirect or misinform, or even to commit sabotage.

Again, this is a frightening thought. It might just mean abductees could be unwitting, and unknowing traitors in our very midst. This is just conjecture and I certainly hope it isn't true. Again, one has to consider all possibilities.

Why do I consider this a possibility? Well, the idea aliens are just performing numerous and repetitive research experiments on the human race in their hundreds of thousands, or even millions, and over and over around the world, just doesn't seem to be too likely a thing to do. One must as, when is enough, enough? At one point, would extraterrestrials have gathered sufficient data for their purposes? Having done this, then why would they continue such abductions?

It would seem far more likely to me and others, as well, that there must be some other reason for why they keep doing this. We can only hope the reason isn't to place such "sleepers" among us for some nefarious purpose. In which case, the old saying, "I have met the enemy and it is us" might just be truer than we ever realized. This is a horrifying thought, indeed.

Is it a realistic one or am I being just unduly pessimistic in even mentioning this idea of sleeper cells hidden amongst the rest of the human population? Well, given that UFOs don't seem to be too benign in their approach to us, our airplanes, or our ships at sea, I don't think it's such a far-fetched idea to think they might have some secret and even dark purpose in returning the abducted to us, often with implants in them, apparently.

Again, there are other possible explanations for why people are being abducted by extraterrestrials. I truly hope one of those is the real reason and not this idea of sleeper cells being planted in our midst. However, I will say this; whatever the reason is for them abducting so many of us, I don't think it's necessarily for our own good. It may be for the extraterrestrials' good, but not necessarily ours, if you get my meaning.

No, these two things might not be the same thing. There is no reason to believe that what might be good for the extraterrestrials is also good for us. After all, this book has pointed out a number of times that such creatures seem not to have the same moral basis, the same belief in basic rights that we do, not at all.

Of course, this lack of such a belief in human rights on their part may be just that, applicable to humans only and so not to them. They may consider that they, as individuals and a species, have certain inalienable rights (no pun intended), but perhaps they simply aren't extending those same rights to us. Maybe, they see us as inferior.

We did this throughout our history, we western nations. None of the European powers prior to World War I, extended the same benefits of citizenship and legal rights to their African colonies. It was the practice not to admit "natives" to European clubs and/or social gatherings, except as servants. "Natives" were not given the benefits under the law the Europeans were. Europeans could seize their lands and pillage them for resources and the native peoples had no choice or say in the matter. So why might not an extraterrestrial species view us all in the same way, as "just local natives" to be used and/or abused as they see fit, something to be exploited?

Their behavior and practices seem to show that this just might be so. Personally, I just don't think that's a good thing, at least, not for us humans now, or for our future as a species. If we are at their mercy, and they have no concept of mercy, such a feeling that might be completely alien to them, then we are in trouble.

CHAPTER 13—CROP CIRCLES

"I can assure you that, given they exist, these flying saucers are made by no power on this Earth."
— **President Harry S. Truman, 4 April 1950**

I will keep this chapter short, as well, because nobody has died in a crop circle, at least not anybody I know of. However, crop circles are so widespread and have been going on for so many decades, perhaps even centuries or millennia that I felt I should at least touch on the subject here. After all, if it is an extraterrestrial phenomenon in some cases, then it forms a part of the puzzle we're facing regarding deadly UFOs and extraterrestrials.

Just how long have crop circles been happening? When did they begin? Well, the answer just might surprise you. There is evidence of crop circles going way back. They have been mentioned as far back as 2000 years ago

However, the first strong evidence for them is the so-called "Mowing Devil." This case occurred in England in 1678. There were reports at the time of some entity, presumably the devil, or at least that's what people believed then, mowed down a large circle in a field of hay. This had such an impact on the locals that a woodblock print was made of the event. A print of this survives to this day.

The phenomenon didn't stop in the year 1678. Robert Plot, in his *A Natural History of Staffordshire,* also talks about strange designs and circles made in various fields in 1686. Moreover, many farmers, ones whose families have farmed the same acreage for countless generations in the United Kingdom, claim that crop circles are nothing new, that their parents and grandparents before them spoke of such things happening. In other words, these farmers felt the phenomenon has always existed. Folklore put it down to supernatural beings, as with the "fairy folk."

There is one thing to consider here, as well. In the 1600s when these events occurred, belief in witches and the devil was real. Charges against women were made and the result was often their torture, deaths, or both. No one took the subject of witchcraft or devil worship lightly in those days! To ridicule such beliefs could mean being challenged as a witch or warlock, and the penalty was often death after a pathetic excuse for a trial. To worship the devil or to be a witch was a capital offense, and the penalty was usually execution.

Why is this important? Well, it means that if there were hoaxes occurring back in those times, they could have very deadly consequences for the perpetrators of them. Additionally, the evidence required to convict someone of witchcraft was often flimsy at best, sometimes little more than an accusation.

So the idea people would be hoaxing crop circles in the 1600s in the dead of night, when they almost certainly would have been declared devil worshipers or witches if caught, seems highly unlikely. One would have had to have a pronounced death wish to do such a thing.

Even the term used for that woodblock print, "Mowing Devil," is proof of just how serious people at the time took such matters. Today, we might practice such hoaxes in the dead of night and in the middle of some farm field. In those days, the fear of being called a witch and/or of undergoing execution would have stopped just about everybody, at least, anybody who was sane. No rational human being would take such a risk to perpetrate such a pointless thing.

Of course, in more recent and modern times, the first real reference to crop circles occurring was in Australia. There, people discovered so-called "UFO Nests" in fields. These circles became known in the latter half of the 1960s. Then, suddenly, the phenomenon exploded and the subject of crop circles became a hot topic in the very late 1970s, and 1980s. It has continued ever since then. Moreover, it is a worldwide phenomenon.

Most of us know by now that some crop circles are the result of hoaxes. This first came out when two men came forward saying they had used a simple contraption of the length of a board with ropes attached to each end to flatten crops in fields, thus creating crop circles. Yet, hoaxes cannot possibly account for all of the crop circles being observed. Why is this so?

1. There are simply too many crop circles happening too often, especially in the United Kingdom, for these to all be hoaxes. To have so many and so often, would mean some perpetrators would be caught by farmers, or the authorities while in the act of doing this, if only by sheer chance. To date, none has been. Yet, to account for all the crop circles occurring, there would have to be hundreds of people involved on a regular basis, many toiling in large numbers all night to create some of the circles seen. This idea seems far-fetched in the extreme.

2. The crop circles have become incredibly intricate. When I say intricate, I mean just that! It has been estimated it would take a large number of people more time than there are hours of darkness to complete just one of those types of circles.

3. Authorities are at a loss as to how to account for all these circles and patterns. Again, despite local efforts to catch the culprits, for damages to crops are no small thing in their eyes, no hoaxers have been caught in the act. Many local officials believe although there are hoaxers out there, they simply cannot account for all the circles made.

Some argue hoaxers get away with their activities because they do them at night and they randomly choose their fields. This markedly lowers their risk of being caught this way.

Yet, England is known for security camera systems. These "CCTV" (Closed Circuit Television) systems are more widespread in the United Kingdom than in any other country in the world. They are so common, they are ubiquitous. In addition, they are everywhere, in the cities, in the villages, along highways — well, again, just about everywhere. Trust me, I know this from firsthand experience. I received a speeding ticket for going four miles over the limit through a tiny village in the middle of nowhere. A camera caught me. Moreover, where they had placed the camera, there was a view of a large farm field, as well. Again, cameras seem to be everywhere in England.

Furthermore, the police and private citizens use these ubiquitous cameras for surveillance purposes in many places. Yet, nothing has ever been seen to be recorded on them as far as people hoaxing crop circles.

There is another factor in all this, as well. Researchers have concluded the crop circles created by human efforts are fundamentally and often blatantly different than those created the "other way." Forensics of the flattened blades of hay or grain, does not show the same characteristics as those flattened by human effort. Joints in the blades of wheat, for instance, are swollen and even burst in some crop circles, but not in those determined to be made by a human agency.

In addition, sphere-like objects have been seen at about the time such crop circles have occurred. There is even video of one moving over a field, passing over the grain and flattening it as it moves along. There is even a farmer in the video, riding a tractor, so the idea this was a faked film, is difficult to believe.

Of course, there are always skeptics about everything who claim that it is still a fake, even so. However, they do not seem to have any basis, any evidence to prove their point. In fact, the reverse seems to be true. The video speaks for itself and they are pushed to account for how it might have been done.

Still, since no one seems to have been killed in a crop circle, again, why do we include them here in our book, which deals primarily with the subject of injuries, deaths and disappearances that are UFO-related?

Well, it would be hard to ignore the question entirely in any book about UFOs. In addition, there might be more sinister connotations to these "signs" in farm fields around the world. People have long conjectured as to what reason they might have to exist. If they aren't all due to hoaxes, and this would seem to be likely, then something else is putting some of those crop circles there.

If so, the question has to be why? In addition, who would do such a thing? Well, considering that UFOs are often sighted in the regions at the time these events occur, there does seem to be a strong connection to the extraterrestrial idea. Yet, we're still left wondering why they would do this?

Well, the answer might just lay in the movie **Signs**, which starred Mel Gibson and Joaquin Phoenix. This science fiction thriller and horror movie proposed the idea that crop circles were a sign, a ground-based navigational system for UFOs to use. Of course, in the movie, it was preparatory to an invasion by extraterrestrials. This might not be the case in real life.

However, it could be a form of temporary navigational system for UFOs, even so. Perhaps the circles are used for guiding such extraterrestrial spacecraft to the various locations of those they wish to abduct? I've seen no study done on this relationship, but it would be interesting to see if there is some statistical correlation in this regard.

Alternatively, perhaps, they are signs to help UFOs more easily travel along ley lines. Again, ley lines are supposed to be a great pattern that encompasses the whole surface of the earth. As previously mentioned, some UFO theorists claim some type of energy yet unknown by our science, flows from them, and alien spacecraft utilize this energy to move around the globe.

I have no idea if this last is true or not, since no such energy has been detected by our scientists. This does not mean it doesn't exist. For most of human history, up until just a little over a century ago, no one, knew x-rays existed, but they did. The same goes for many other types of radiation, including gamma, ultraviolet, infrared, microwave radiation and more.

Just because our science was incapable of perceiving such forms of energy until fairly recently, didn't mean they did not exist. Therefore, the same may hold true for ley lines.

In any case, that these elaborate patterns in farm fields, which we refer to collectively as crop circles, exist, is not in doubt. That they can't possibly all be hoaxes, also is not in doubt. Furthermore, that UFOs have been seen near areas where crop circles occur is also true. Just what the reason for the circles existence, for being created, is, we can only conjecture.

Nevertheless, if extraterrestrials are sane, they must have a reason for making them. Other than some sort of elaborate cosmic joke being played upon us, we have to conclude there must be some rational purpose why they would go through the trouble of creating crop circles.

It is our not knowing the reason that makes it rather frightening for us. Are they just playful designs in the fields, made by precocious extraterrestrials committing practical jokes upon us just for the fun of it? Alternatively, is the reason for their existence something darker, possibly even something malevolent as portrayed in the movie, **Signs**? Again, we just don't know. Perhaps, we should make more of an effort to find out, given the possible implications of crop circles? And do remember the consultant to the movie died not long after under mysterious circumstances…

CHAPTER 14—ANIMAL MUTILATIONS

"Of course the flying saucers are real and they are interplanetary...The cumulative evidence for the existence of UFOs is quite overwhelming and I accept the fact of their existence."
— **Air Chief Marshal Lord Dowding, RAF, August 1954**

We've all heard about animal mutilations. They occur in their thousands. Nobody seems to know why. However, the UFO world is rife with suggestions, possible explanations, and conspiracy theories regarding such terrible events. It doesn't matter what kind of animal, whether bovine or equine, or whatever, these abominations occur often, on an annual basis, and in great numbers. Animals seem to have parts of them surgically removed. Whether Wyoming, Nebraska, California, Manitoba, Saskatchewan, England, or elsewhere it's the same story over and over. Animals are killed. Portions of their anatomy are surgically removed.

Some say this surgery is with laser-like precision. Whether the anus, the tongue, uterus, eyes or whatever, there is almost no bleeding involved. It's as if the wounds were self-cauterized. Moreover, UFOs have often been sighted around the time such events occur. Strangely, not only UFOs are seen, but silent helicopters. Black ones in color and without any kind of official numbering or lettering on them, are also seen at times when such events occur. Although they have no noise, other than perhaps a faint humming sound, there is still the noise of the accompanying rush of air the blades cause, as well as their lights to help witnesses spot them.

The important thing here is the mutilations, themselves. They seem to occur everywhere, as well. It isn't just the North American continent suffering from such atrocities in their thousands. The problem seems to be truly a global one.

Since many of us have heard and read so much about what goes on in North America with regard to such inexplicable treatment of our animals, I feel the subject in that regard has been fairly well covered by others. However, no book about the deadly nature of UFOs can be complete without mentioning the subject.

Additionally, since many here in the United States are not aware of what goes on elsewhere in the world in this regard, I thought I would focus here in this book on the United Kingdom, specifically with a very bizarre event that took place there. This is to show that animal mutilations do not stop at borders, whether Canadian, American, British, Australian, or anywhere else in the world. All these countries, too, have seen such events take place, and again, in great numbers. Never did the authorities in any of these places seem to have satisfactory explanations to account for them, either.

A strange event involving sheep took place in the United Kingdom. In addition, based on *The Daily Telegraph* newspaper article published at the time, as well as others. Here's a more concise report of those events:

Shropshire, England, United Kingdom, April 2010. Farmers in the area were upset. They were concerned by a number of unexplained killings of their sheep, felt the cause was UFO related. The authorities claimed such an idea was just jumping to wrong conclusions, and/or "wild conspiracy theories."

However, a team of private investigators disagreed. They based their conclusion on their investigations of the whole matter. They checked out numerous deaths of animals and not only in Shropshire, but Wales, as well. They stated that farmers in those regions had complained of animal deaths under strange circumstances for over a decade prior to the current spate of events.

These deaths, or animal attacks, as they referred to them, had taken place over a wide area. This region included Knighton, Gwynedd, Powys, and Beddgelert, among others. Furthermore, these investigators, who refer to themselves as the Animal Pathology Field Unit, doubt the government or any sort of military is involved in these events, not based on what they've discovered, it seems.

No less than 15 investigators kept up surveillance of a farm in the hills near Radnor, Powys. They reported saying two floating/flying spheres, red in color, passed swiftly over the landscape there. They claim the spheres could change shape, "morph" into various other ones. Afterwards, the investigators discovered farmers had found some of their livestock had undergone mutilations. Principally, these were sheep. The types of mutilations were the same as in other regions around the world. These included holes in their skulls and brains, the extraction of various internal organs, as well as missing eyes, and sometimes, the flesh of the animals had been removed.

Nor can the investigators come up with any sort of standard or rational explanation for such strange occurrences. They could find no normal possible cause. If no "possible" explanation can be found, then this can only lead to the conclusion the explanation must be an "impossible" one, as the fictional character, Sherlock Holmes was wont to say. Their conclusion: they were dealing with some kind of strange intelligence, and/or technology well beyond the capabilities of any human civilization on Earth.

This was despite the group's efforts to first find a more logical and mundane reason for the events. As a matter of course, they knew many lambs would die each season, for instance. This would be due to a variety of natural factors, including disease, predation, unseasonable weather, etc. Therefore, they investigated such possible causes. However, the mutilations were not the product of attacks by dogs, badgers, or any other known animal in the area.

The idea of the animals being killed for satanic rituals also came up. However, nobody could explain how such people might do such a neat, cauterized job of removing such internal organs and creating such types of mutilations with any currently known means. They ruled this cause out as a possible one.

Furthermore, the animals were examined for evidence, that after their deaths, some other type of creature might have caused the weird mutilations. They looked to scavengers as an explanation.

This was a fruitless endeavor, as well, as it turned out. Creatures such as rats, crows, or ravens, or any other such type of scavenger just didn't seem at all likely to have caused such types of wounds. The fact was, in many cases, it would have been impossible according to the investigators. The precision of some of the injuries was just too perfect for any animal, let alone a crow for example, to have caused. One investigator reported that the missing organs looked as if they had been "clinically removed."

Again, this should sound familiar to those of us in North America. It is the same pattern repeated here and elsewhere. It is a pattern repeated worldwide and every single year. Countless deaths of livestock keep occurring. Nobody seems to know the cause. At least, no authority or government agency is willing to admit to a cause.

The investigators also pointed out that horses on the moors, in Dartmoor, as well as some badger mutilations along the entire east coast of England, had similar characteristics in their deaths at times. The same thing held true for some hedgehogs in Yorkshire, England, as well. So sometimes, even the so-called scavengers of the livestock are victims of the same types of mutilations.

Are UFOs involved in all of this? It would seem likely. At a stakeout near the Radnorshire forest, some investigators said they saw what "looked more like a Star Wars battle in the skies. This event started with a red glowing object hovering low in the distance, or the edge of the forest. The investigators assumed it was a light from a home, but this proved not to be the case. As they continued to watch. They realized the light couldn't be any land-based source, because it was too far off the ground. Moreover, another and similar red light appeared close to the first one.

The investigators further claimed the lights began to change shape, as well as emitting spheres of light from them. The small spheres moved about the landscape, low to the ground, and one investigator said it was as if they were looking for something. To complicate matters further, the investigators said beams of light shot out from various areas within the forest, as if attacking the spheres. The researchers said the whole affair had the distinct look of a battle of some strange sort.

Then, one of the two red spheres winked out and then reappeared off to the investigators' right, over a small hill near where they were camped. They witnessed a beam of white light shine down the hill in their direction. As one investigator put it, *"I thought the red spheres knew we were there, that they were watching us."*

Since this went on for some time, the researchers had a chance to study and to try to identify the phenomena. They couldn't. No natural explanation seemed to apply. The objects were not any sort of known meteorological phenomenon, nor were they Chinese lanterns, or paper bags with candles inside of them floating into the air. They did not behave in any such fashion, did not drift about randomly, and certainly no such objects as those could emit beams of light, as these things did. Nor did they behave or appear as if they were ball lightning.

Investigators also said these sort of events seemed to cluster in a well-defined region, or as they put it, *"a 50-mile corridor."* This corridor lay between Shrewsbury and Powys. However, they say such events also take place on Dartmoor (as with the horses there), as well as near Gloucestershire in the Forest of Dean. The same sort of mutilations occur there, as well.

Nor did these mutilations stop. They have continued for over 12 years and might have been going on much longer. However, the investigators could only personally account for the time they were actually researching these events, so they couldn't say for sure.

Not only investigators witnessed such things, but other people, as well. Many witnesses reported sighting light displays in and around that same "corridor" near Shropshire. Numerous reports of orange-colored spheres flying about also flooded in during that time. People in cars lining the highways have seen lights in the night sky, with white or red beams shooting down from them at times.

Sometimes, the groups of witnesses have been large, with cars, even pulling over to the side of the road and creating traffic jams to watch the displays. Nobody seemed to know what caused those, either. Witnesses even included police officers, as well as a retired police officer and his spouse. He claims he and his wife saw six glowing spheres seemingly flying in some sort of formation, pass right over his home.

Near Radnor, a constable, along with his partner, also spotted such a sphere. He claims the glowing globe caused damage to his police vehicle, to both the sign and light on the top of his car. This is very reminiscent of another case in the United States where an officer had his car damaged, as well, if you will remember.

One witness told of how he saw a sphere of orange light hovering over some small pools of water. He said he had "*the distinct impression*" the sphere was sucking water from these pools. Again, this is reminiscent of the ranch hand who reported much the same thing with regard to the ranch's water tank in Australia. Yet this was half a world away from there. He then said the sphere then shot away at an incredible velocity, flying upwards until it vanished into the sky.

He was not the only person to see such a thing. A scientist also saw something similar, early one morning. Strangely, these events always seem to occur at about that same time, between 12 AM and 2 AM in the morning.

So do these glowing spheres of light have something to do with the mutilations of livestock and other animals? Yes, they seem to, because they have appeared regularly around the very regions were such mutilations have occurred and at the time of such occurrences. At the very least, there seems a direct correlation between the two phenomena, if only because of this "coincidence" of UFO sightings seen so often where people discover the corpses of mutilated animals.

So what can we make of this? These mutilations in the United Kingdom are very much in line with those in other regions around the world. The descriptions of the types of mutilations, the observing of UFOs around the times and locales of such mutilations, all give credence to the idea the two phenomenon are connected. This seems to be a more than reasonable assumption.

So what is going on? Why are so many countless animals being brutally murdered, and killed in such awful ways? By most countries' standards, such animal deaths are akin to a form of torture. In America, for example, there are criminal statutes against doing this sort of thing to animals in many regions of the country. Moreover, the fact this is a worldwide problem is also a given. Where there are mutilations, there also seem to be UFO sightings.

From this, I can only conclude, given this massive amount of evidence, UFOs have some direct connection to such animal deaths. If this is so, then not only are UFOs unfriendly towards humans, but they seem manifestly unfriendly towards our animals, as well. Extraterrestrials seem to have no compunction about killing livestock and other creatures, and in great numbers. They seem to take what they want, for whatever strange reasons, and without any sense that what they're doing is wrong.

In short, they kill animals without compunction or compassion. If, as some contactees claim, extraterrestrials are our "space brothers," then one is hard-pressed to understand why our "space brothers" would do such a terrible thing, keep on doing it, and in such massive numbers.

One has to ask the question: what is going on? This I can't answer, but I do know one thing, and that is, something is definitely going on. That "something" doesn't appear to be good. At least, it's not good to those thousands upon thousands of animals that are being butchered in such horrible ways. It's not good for the farmers and ranchers who own many of these animals.

The conclusion of this section on animal mutilations? Well, extraterrestrials, or whatever they are, are damaging our environment and ecology. They seem to have no moral problems in doing this. They commit such killings when they want, how they want, and where they want. That "where" is worldwide. These countless animal mutilations seem to be part of an overall pattern of negative UFO behavior toward us and ours. Again, and again, we see repeated examples of damage, injuries, and death involved where UFOs are concerned.

When it comes to animal mutilations by extraterrestrials, this only adds to an already powerful body of evidence for my case that UFOs are a "clear and present danger" to us humans, and perhaps an equal threat to the other creatures of this Earth. Nor does the evidence end here. There is even more.

PART 4—MYSTERY OF THE DISAPPEARED!

"People simply disappeared, always during the night."
—**George Orwell,** *1984*

CHAPTER 15—THE DISAPPEARED—INDIVIDUALS

"We all know that UFOs are real. All we need to ask is where do they come from."
—**Astronaut Edgar D. Mitchell**

People disappear all the time. They disappear and in all sorts of ways. Moreover, they disappear in great numbers. In the United States alone, it is estimated anywhere from 800,000 to 1,000,000 people vanish each year. This number may seem high, but given our population is now over 300 million, it really isn't so out of line as one might think.

Of course, most of the people who disappear do so for the normal sort of "everyday" reasons. Many want just to vanish. This may be because of a heavy burden of debts, of trying to get out of relationships they no longer want, or simply to start a new and fresh existence under a different and assumed identity elsewhere. Many disappearances, in fact the majority, are young people, teenagers and adolescents who just run away from home for whatever reasons.

Furthermore, there are kidnappings, as well. Separated parents will sometimes try to snatch a child from the other one when they are fighting over custody issues, and then abscond with the child. Therefore, there are a number of normal reasons for disappearances of people. Yet, although 93 to 95 percent of these cases are explainable in this way, there is still that nagging 5 to 8 percent which we cannot explain with any of these reasons.

Some people simply vanish from existence, it seems. Often, they do so under incredibly strange circumstances and without a trace. This, apparently, has always been happening throughout history. There are reports of ancient Romans, ancient Greeks, and others who have disappeared.

Again, many of these can be explained away as kidnappings, being captured in battles, or whatever. However, there are some few, again, which don't fall under these explanations.

With the ancient disappearances, they happened so long ago we have no way of investigating them, of knowing for sure what happened to these disappeared individuals. Those disappearances are what they are. So any skeptic can claim whatever they like about them, since there is no real evidence either way to support one viewpoint over another, except people have always disappeared.

However, in the case of more recent vanishings, we do have more evidence to substantiate what might have happened to some of the disappeared, or more correctly, what did not happen to them. This is because of the circumstances under which the people disappeared, the events surrounding the disappearances.

Over the decades, there are thousands of such cases just in the United States alone. That number I quoted who disappeared in the United States, again, 800,000 to 1,000,000 per year, only includes Americans residing in the country. The figures do not include citizens of the United States who vanish overseas or those missing cases that simply aren't reported to the authorities for whatever reasons. However, other countries also report disappearances. Australia, for instance, by one figure, has about 35,000 people who vanish there every year. As countries go, Australia doesn't have a large population, comparatively speaking (just over 23 million). Therefore, this number would seem large to us.

Apparently, it seems large to other people, as well. Committees, both national and international ones, have been organized to try to deal with this issue. For instance, the International Commission on Missing Persons is just one example of those endeavoring to handle the large number of people who have disappeared.

Again, these disappearances go back a long ways. There are many of them. Here, just as examples, are some of the more reliable accounts to illustrate this fact:

Owen Parfitt, 1763 or 1768 (date is argued). Owen Parfitt, an Englishman, lived a very colorful life, which apparently included a large number of tales, some undoubtedly tall tales, about his exciting youth. These stories included everything from being involved in battles, making love to many beautiful women, and even incidents with vicious pirates. Whether these tales are true or not are probably a moot point, because he did lead am extreme sort of life by most people's reckoning of the day. Moreover, his end was even more memorable.

As with all things, the good times couldn't last for Owen forever, it seemed. As he grew older, he became increasingly feeble. By the time he was in his sixties, he could barely move about at all. He had deteriorated to a state that left him in a crippled condition.

This meant he could no longer live alone, and so he had to move in with a sister in the town of Shepton Mallet in the United Kingdom. This was in the 1760's although the exact date is a subject for debate. Some say what followed occurred in 1763, while others say 1768. Even so, the details of what happened next are clear and remain the same.

Owen's sister had allowed him to sit outside one evening, it being rare good weather. This had required not only her efforts to move him, but that of a neighbor, as well. He was on the front porch, where he could sit and enjoy the early evening. His sister left him there and returned indoors.

There were some people not far away, a small group of farm laborers, who Owen could have called to for help if he needed it for some emergency. They were close enough easily to view him. Because the weather started turning for the worse, his sister decided that it was time for her brother to come inside again. She went out onto the porch to tell him this.

Unfortunately, Owen was no longer there. He had vanished. The nearby farm laborers, as well as the local neighbors, all helped to search for him. However, of Owen, they could find nothing. A man who had to be carried in order to be moved about, had somehow disappeared from the front porch of his sister's home never to be found again. He had simply vanished.

Of course, legends grew, such as he had been snatched by Satan, or perhaps had been kidnapped by pirates. Still, nothing ever came of these and the problem remained that the nearby workers should easily have witnessed such an event, any sort of such ruckus, and/or that Owen could have called out to them for help in such dire circumstances. They saw nothing and they heard nothing. Only his coat remained on his chair.

Later, in 1813, a skeleton was discovered in the nearby town of Shepton Mallet, but this proved to be the remains of a young woman, and not a man. To this day, nobody knows what happened to that crippled old man who had been dozing on the front porch of his sister's home early one evening.

Diderici, Danzig, Prussia, 1815. Danzig, now a part of present-day Poland, was where a one-time valet for a Prussian Army officer assumed the soldier's identity upon his demise. This worked out well for a while, because this gave the valet a lifestyle he could never have afforded otherwise. Things were good for him and looking better.

However, again as with most good things, the idyllic times had to end for Diderici. He ended up by being tried and incarcerated in Danzig Wiechselmunde Prison for identity theft and the using of a dead man's funds to make his own life better. As told in the book, *Lost And Never Found Two*, by the author, Anita Larsen, other prisoners swore that Diderici, while walking one day in the fenced prison yard for exercise, simply slowly faded from view until he disappeared completely.

Later, some skeptics of this version said he must have somehow freed himself from his shackles and so disappeared into the mist and fog that might have been prevalent that day. However, although as down-to-earth as this version might appear, it does not coincide with what the other prisoners said, nor is there any evidence there was fog that day.

Furthermore, it doesn't explain how he managed to escape the confinement of the prison grounds or his shackles, and thus disappearing without trace. Nobody ever saw him again, never witnessed him as being alive after that event, at least not those who might recognize him. To this day, the case has never been satisfactorily resolved. Diderici simply vanished.

William Morgan, 1826. William Morgan had a thing about the Free Masons. He feared them and apparently despised them as well. He also claimed to have an intimate knowledge of them. In 1826, he stated he was going to publish a book, one that would make public all the secrets he had learned while having been involved with them.

Morgan found himself arrested shortly after saying this and not just once, but twice on the flimsiest of excuses. On one of the occasions, even the judge said it just was a *"trumped up charge."*

Then two men paid the several dollars to free him from prison in Canandaigua, New York, and as they took him outside, some locals heard him shout "murder" several times. He was then loaded into a carriage. He was never seen again.

Who were the two men who had paid his bail? Were they Free Masons intent on murdering Morgan? Why has not anyone ever discovered his body in all this time, if this was so? What was so important to the Free Masons if murder had been their intent with regard to William Morgan? Truly, what secrets of the Free Masons could have been so important as to commit such a deed?

We are assured repeatedly today that Free Masons have nothing to hide. Yet, some argue they do, that they are associated with the truly ancient cult group, the Brotherhood of the Snake, which is said by some to have secret knowledge handed down to them by extraterrestrials. Was Morgan about to reveal some of this knowledge? As it stands, it seems we will never know. Morgan simply vanished, and this time, it appears a human agency might have been involved.

James Worson, 1873. This is an exceedingly strange case, because of the number of eyewitnesses involved and the unusual circumstances. James Worson, a resident of Leamington Spa in the United Kingdom, and as the result of a gambling bet with his companions, decided to prove his boast about his prowess as a runner. To insure the validity of the results, as James ran, his friends and compatriots rode in a horse cart, intent on keeping a close eye on James. It appears they may have felt he might cheat, if they did not do this.

After several miles, they saw James appear to trip. He tumbled forward and fell facedown, toward the ground. Here is the weird part of this; the witnesses all claimed he never made it to the ground. He literally vanished as he fell. Not believing this was possible, his friends scoured the area looking for him, checking for all possible alternatives to what they had seen.

They never found him. James Worson had disappeared from the face of the Earth. Even police investigations failed to uncover any other facts about the event. James Worson had not only vanished, but he had vanished forever, seemingly.

Charles Ashmore, 1878. A youth of sixteen, Charles Ashmore, who lived in Quincy, Illinois, went to the well to draw water. This was at night in November, and being cold, the family assumed he would not tarry long outside in such an endeavor, but would speedily return.

Charles did not. In fact, his family never saw him again, for he simply seemed to have vanished. Fearing the worst, the family frantically searched for him, afraid he may have fallen into the well. He did not, for despite a thorough investigation, they never discovered any trace of his body.

However, they did see his footprints clearly in the snow stopping abruptly midway toward the well. There were no other footprints around his, nothing, either animal or human. It was as if something had plucked him from the ground and up into the air. Despite all his family's frantic and determined efforts to find him, they never saw Charles again, nor did they find any remains. He had simply vanished, just as so many others had vanished before him.

Dorothy Arnold, December 1910. She disappeared while taking a walk in Central Park on December 12, 1910. She simply vanished. For someone so famous as she was to disappear under such circumstances today would have caused a worldwide media sensation, Dorothy was famous, being the daughter of a well-to-do perfume importer, as well as the niece of an Associate Justice of the Supreme Court, no less. She was a highly sought after socialite on the New York scene of the day.

Of course, rumors abounded about what might have happened to her, but the authorities discovered nothing of any real evidence in any way. They found no clues of any sort whatsoever, or any remains. She had simply vanished forever.

Ambrose Bierce, 1914. This is an odd story. Here is a man who was an author, as well as a journalist. One of his short stories was about a farmer who disappeared in mid-step while crossing a field in front of eyewitnesses. This story has taken on the proportions of an urban or rather rural legend. People now believe it actually happened, but it did not. The name of the farmer and his family has never been associated with the area where this was supposed to have happened. There are no newspaper records of such an event occurring. Therefore, one can only assume this was a story that he portrayed as fact when it was not. Yet, later in life, as an aging journalist, he went to Mexico where he traveled with troops rebelling against the Mexican government in 1914. He disappeared. His place of disappearance was somewhere in Chihuahua, Mexico.

Of course, many assumed he was killed in some fashion. Perhaps he was. If so, nobody has discovered his body. Despite repeated attempts to locate the remains, and other bodies having been found, none of them belonged to Ambrose Bierce. Neither he nor his belongings have ever been discovered, and this, despite the fact people have followed his actual trail of travel and more than once in hopes of finding something.

Nor do the rebels with whom he traveled have an explanation for his disappearance. They claim no responsibility for his vanishing and/or death. He was liked by them. They felt he would share his story of their struggle for freedom. In other words, they had no cause to kill him. It was quite the contrary, in fact.

It is singularly odd that a man, who should write a story about someone vanishing from the face of the Earth, should himself then disappear in such a way. It is quite the coincidence. Was his earlier story actually genuine? Had he reported something that might have actually happened, only to then have it happen to him as a result? We probably will never know.

Later in the twentieth century, such famous people as **Amelia Earhart, Glenn Miller, Jimmy Hoffa**, and many others also vanished. Although rumors and legends abound about them, as well, as to what have might have happened to them, nobody seems to know. All they have are suppositions and little else.

However, the number of disappeared throughout the twentieth century is not a small one. Although how they disappeared, the circumstances under which they vanished differed from person to person, they all have one thing in common: they have never been seen again, not alive and not dead.

In modern times, this seems very hard to understand. With the available technology at our disposal, and the sheer number of people who have looked for the bodies of such persons, one simply can't understand how this could be. Why can no one come up with anything concrete in this regard? Despite people who have made claims to knowing where bodies might be, and this happening repeatedly, no bodies have ever been discovered in such cases, as with Jimmy Hoffa, who if one believes various criminals, was buried near a barn on a farm, or in the concrete of a stadium, etc. Despite all these claims and repeated expensive investigations, his remains have never been located.

So-called Bennington Triangle, 1940's to 1950's. In the area of Bennington, Vermont, later referred to by one radio announcer as the "Bennington Triangle, there were a number of weird disappearances. In the span of just five years, five individuals vanished from this immediate region, which is a rural one.

Middie Rivers, November 1945. Middie, a 74-year-old, simply vanished while out hunting with four other people. It was on the return from this outing that Rivers disappeared. Middie Rivers had ranged slightly ahead of the other four in their hike back to home, and this was when the disappearance took place. Again, as with other such cases, a thorough and meticulous search for Middie ensued. This was near the Long Trail Road. They found nothing.

It's hard to account for this disappearance, because as with other and similar cases, there was no sign of foul play. Additionally, Middie was experienced in the area where he disappeared, knew the locale well, had long been a hunter there. Therefore, investigators are at a loss as to what might have occurred to cause the disappearance. To this day, nobody has found any sign of a body. Middie Rivers simply vanished.

Paula Welden, December 1946. Paula Weldon, aged 18, hiked the Long Trail at Glastonbury Mountain in this same region as Middie Rivers. Following close behind her on that same trail was an older couple, no more than 100 yards from her, at most.

Paula went out of sight around a rocky mound. Moments later, the couple reached the same spot. They fully expected to sight Paula Welden again up ahead of them, but of the young woman, there now was no sign, nothing. Despite an exhaustive search by authorities, nobody ever saw her again. They never found any remains. Again, like all those others before her, she had vanished forever.

Nor were any of her belonging ever discovered. It is such events as these, in the Long Trail area, that have made many believe something like a Bigfoot might have been involved. Still, no tracks of any such a creature were discovered in the vicinities of the disappearances, although often, there have been tracks of those who vanished. Again, there was no sign of foul play, or any cries for help, which the couple would certainly have heard. The disappearance is just another enigma, one of many such.

James Tetford, December 1949. Domiciled in a soldier's home in Bennington, Vermont, aging resident James Tetford vanished while traveling on a bus. There were fourteen other passengers also journeying on the vehicle at the time, so the bus had quite a number of fellow occupants aboard at the time of his disappearance. These passengers all claimed to have seen him there, sitting on the bus alongside of them. Many said he had been sleeping in his seat.

However, when the vehicle arrived at its destination, of Mr. Tetford, there was no sign at all. He had simply vanished. However, as further corroboration he had been aboard, his actual presence there, all of his luggage was still there, as well, and a timetable for busses was found on his seat. No one ever discovered him or his remains. He has vanished forever.

Paul Jepson, October 1950. The young boy, Paul Jepson lived on a farm. As was her usual practice, Paul's mother let him outside to play for a while. She did this while she attended to the needs of various animals on the farm. However, this time when she returned, she found no sign of her son. He, like so many others, had simply vanished. They mounted searches for the boy. Authorities conducted investigations. All of these were to no avail. Again, young Paul had simply disappeared. Nobody ever found any remains of the child. Thus, with these disappearances, we have the birth of the mysterious Bennington Triangle, so-called.

We must remember just how rural this area was. Crime was virtually nonexistent there, certainly almost nothing of a serious nature. The idea someone abducted all these people, in the sense of being kidnapped by criminals, would seem highly unlikely. Surely, the remains of at least some of them should have been found later? This never happened.

Additionally, the circumstances of many of these incidents would seem to rule out that idea, of kidnapping. Yes, it is conceivable one or two of them might have been kidnapped, but all of them, including an old man from a soldiers' home and right off of a crowded bus? This just doesn't seem to be a very likely thing to have happen. Something else must be at work here. Certainly, Bigfoot wasn't responsible for that particular disappearance. So who was? Better yet, what was?

Nor did these types of incidents, these vanishings stop here. They continued. Even as they had gone on for centuries before, they didn't slow down at this point. There are yet more examples with which to contend in this regard.

Martha Wright, New York, 1975. While passing through the Lincoln Tunnel on his way from New Jersey to New York, Jackson Wright had trouble with condensation forming on the interior windshield of his car. This became so bad he had trouble seeing. Forced to pull over for safety reasons, he and his wife, Martha, exited the vehicle to clear the windows. Jackson saw to wiping the windshield while his wife took care of the rear window.

When having finished his brief task, Jackson turned to his wife. He could find no sign of her. She had vanished. Furthermore, there had been no sign anything was amiss, either prior to their stopping, or during the wiping of the windows. Jackson had heard nothing, seen nothing. A subsequent investigation on his part could find no evidence of foul play. His wife had simply vanished. She wasn't in the tunnel and there certainly hadn't been time for her to exit the shaft. Anyone who has driven the Holland or Lincoln Tunnels knows they are not short ones.

Martha Wright had just vanished. Later, a police investigation could find no evidence of anything, let alone wrongdoing on the part of Jackson Wright. Again, Martha Wright, like so many before her, had simply disappeared under inexplicable circumstances. Nobody saw her again. They found nothing in the way of remains.

Frederick Valentich, 1978. As mentioned earlier, Frederick disappeared while flying his Cessna plane in southern Australia over a narrow strait there. He had reported seeing UFOs and the fact they were interfering with his flight.

Then he vanished from the face of the Earth, also never to be seen again. I mention him here, as well as earlier on, because his was a bona fide disappearance. The numbers of people disappearing in this way, with UFOs seen nearby at the time, are more than you might imagine. Entire books, and series of books, have been written on the subject of disappearances.

As just one current example, there is Author, David Paulides, with his *Missing 411* books, which delve into the many regional disappearances of people, especially those in isolated or rural regions, such as our national and state parks. What seems to bother this author greatly is the fact of the disappearances and that the national park system seems deliberately to hide this problem. At the very least, they do not publicize the problem to any degree whatsoever.

David seems to feel this is wrong, because people should be warned if there are dangers, especially unknown dangers to be faced in such so-called recreational areas. Although the author never actually explains what he thinks the source of so many disappearances might be, besides the obvious ones of people getting lost and dying, he does seem to infer throughout his books that the cause may be something in nature itself.

We're not just talking about the ordinary types of wild beasts, such as bears and mountain lions, as one would expect here. He seems to hint around the idea of something like a Bigfoot being one of the possible causes. One cannot read his books without feeling the dark presence of this idea lurking somewhere in the background, although again, he does not state this openly.

These disappearances have been an ongoing problem for decades. People report missing relatives and friends all over the United States in our national parks. The Appalachian Trail seems to be one of the worst affected areas for this deadly sort of thing. Adults and children, both, vanish there without a trace. Such was the case with Dennis Martin.

Dennis Martin, 1969. Just six years old, Dennis disappeared in the Great Smoky Mountains National Park. This was in an area called Cades Cove, Tennessee. This also took place along the Appalachian Trail there, which stretches most of the way up and down the east coast of the United States. His disappearance was sudden, and took place in a very short space of time. He, as we've mentioned quite a number of times with others now, vanished without a trace. They haven't found him or any of his remains. Therefore, for the grieving family, there has been no closure in this regard.

These vanishings are an ongoing phenomenon. Even now, people disappear in our parks. Here is a more recent example:

Carl Landers, 1999. Along with a two other men, Carl Landers wanted to hike to the summit of Mount Shasta. His companions were his friends, Barry Gillmore and Milt Gaines. The three made camp before reaching Lake Helen, which was on the way. They had decided to take a break there, before ascending to the peak the next day.

However, Carl, claiming not to feel the best, decided to go ahead, so that he could proceed more slowly, rather than having to struggle trying to keep up with his comrades all the next day. He wanted to cover some more ground, so that on the morrow things might be easier for him in the final push for the top of the peak, which he knew would be arduous.

Carl never made it. He vanished. They were unable to find any trace of him or any of his camping equipment/gear, or anything else, for that matter. It's as if he just disappeared from the face of the Earth and took all his belongings with him. Carl was an experienced hiker and climber. This was not a novice attempting to achieve something beyond his capabilities.

Rosemary Kunst, 2000. Another intriguing case is that of a San Anselmo woman. Rosemary Kunst, grieving for her dead husband, decided to go on a spiritual retreat in an attempt to find some peace and come to terms with her loss. This, she decided to do in the Marble Mountain area, near Spirit Lake,

California. When the group's guide and leader suggested they hike farther, Rosemary demurred. She wished to stay and enjoy the serenity of Spirit Lake. This she did.

However, after a while, Rosemary was seized with the idea of taking a walk along the edge of the lake. A young man, who had elected to remain behind as well, did not wish to make the journey with her, so Rosemary went alone.

Rosemary never returned. She simply seemed to have vanished. Despite an extensive air and ground search in an attempt to find her, nothing was ever recovered. The seventy-year-old woman was just gone. There wasn't any question of a struggle, for there was no blood, nothing. Everything she had disappeared along with her. Even the packed lunch she had taken, vanished. Furthermore, the police had no reason to suspect she had been the victim of any sort of crime or that she had taken her own life. Even if she had, where was the body?

Gerry Lagray, July 2013. A woman by the name of Gerry Lagray, while hiking along the Appalachian Trail in Maine, simply disappeared forever. Moreover, she did have company for much of the time, so it was not as if she had been entirely alone for her whole journey. Not being a novice at hiking, she had made friends with other hikers, and groups who were walking the trail. In emergencies, these sorts of temporary bonds with fellow travelers can be useful, of help. Gerry had also arranged to meet up with her husband on a regular basis so she he could restock her supplies when they became low.

Then, while traversing a particularly difficult area of the trail in Maine, on a segment of the trip, which would take three days before she again met up with her husband, she vanished, never to be seen again. They never recovered her or any of her belongings.

As we have seen, this problem isn't restricted to just the east coast of the United States, and our national parks there. Again, vanishing people occur all over America. So it goes and continues to go. The list of such odd disappearances just keeps growing. Repeatedly, this sort of thing has happened. Repeatedly, it continues to happen, and we have no hope it will stop any time soon.

Moreover, the numbers are frightening, to say the very least. According to some estimates, the number is in the high hundreds, even the thousands and still the disappearances don't let up. Every year, it seems, people vanish from national and state parks somewhere in our country. In many cases, we have no idea what happened to them.

The idea that it might be a creature like Bigfoot, or Sasquatch, is a legitimate consideration. After all, these are wild areas. When one ventures far into them, one is isolated and alone, sometimes for days at a time. Perhaps such creatures do exist, if sparely, in such wild and remote places. There seems to be some evidence for this. So, is it likely something like a Bigfoot is responsible for the disappearances of many of these people? Let's consider the matter:

The majority of cases of disappearances seem to be complete ones. This means that often nothing of the person or their belongings ever becomes known. Often, there are no remains discovered. Is a Bigfoot eating these people? Well, if it is, it seems it consumes them bag and baggage, because all of their equipment usually disappears along with them, including bedrolls, knapsacks, hiking sticks, cooking equipment, toiletries—you name it — it disappears forever, as well.

So how do we account for this if it is Bigfoot attacking and eating people? Do the creatures use camp stoves, sleeping bags, canteens, and various medications, and so abscond with these items, as well? Do they hide them somewhere in the woods for later use on their own? This proposition would seem manifestly unlikely in the extreme. Why would they need cooking equipment, for example, if they're consuming people raw? Moreover, we've seen no sign of mysterious cooking fires in such isolated regions of the park, at least, none that can't be accounted for as having normal origins.

Secondly, there is the problem of a lack of footprints. Often, the footprints of the person are there and then they just stop. Nothing is around them, no footprints of anything else. Not animals, not people, and certainly, there are no signs of a Bigfoot's tracks.

So how do we explain this? Why are there no footprints corresponding to those of a Bigfoot or Sasquatch also seen along with the tracks of the person in such disappearances? After all, the creature is much larger than humans are supposed to be, if one is to believe the descriptions of the monster. So shouldn't their footprints be even more pronounced than those of humans they take? Yet, none seems to be found.

Of course, forest rangers could be hiding the fact of such footprints, but this would seem hard to believe. The National Park Service may have a policy of not mentioning such disappearances of people within its parks, so as not to lower the number of tourists in attendance there each year, but it would be quite a stretch to think they were actively colluding in a cover-up of evidence with regard to such footprints. These people are forest rangers, after all, and not members of the CIA or some other clandestine government organization. In any case, wouldn't there be some talk of this, some dissemination of this information by them to their families and friends through the rumor mill, if only after they've retired? There seems to be none of this happening.

So if these total disappearances, humans, along with bag and baggage, are sometimes taking place in very short spans of time, often involving people who are exceptional healthy, are indeed happening, then just how are they vanishing? There are a number of answers to this question. Some seem more likely than others do.

If the usual explanations of accidents, kidnappings, death by animals don't fit, perhaps the person could simply be walking into a different dimension? Could they have somehow stumbled through a time warp? Perhaps they entered a parallel universe? I don't discount this possibility, although I don't think it a great probability. There is little evidence to suggest this as the reason.

Why would such things only occur in our national park system and to such an extent? It would seem unlikely. Even so, one can't discount the idea entirely. The universe has more unanswered questions for us still, than answered ones. So who really knows? Still, I think this being the reason has a low probability.

Why do I say this? Well, when these people disappear, they are alone. Nobody seems to witness the event. It's almost as if the event of their vanishing coincides too neatly with the fact they are alone and isolated at the time of its occurrence. Therefore, whatever is happening to them seems to be deliberate, as if someone or something is taking advantage of their isolation, however temporary it may be.

For this reason, random fluctuations in our spacetime would not seem to be the answer. Because if so, why don't these disappearances happen with equal frequency everywhere? They should not just occur under such specific circumstances or locations. Why don't they take place just as frequently in urban areas, for instance? They don't seem to. No, I don't rule out the possibility of entering such alternate realities as being the reason, but again and for the conditions mentioned, I think it less likely, at least for most such cases we've stated heretofore.

However, I'm sure this is why some people think it might be a Bigfoot sort of creature doing this, some creature waiting for its opportunity to seize the victims when nobody else is about the place to help them. This is a distinct possibility and a more likely one for me. Nevertheless, if so, where is the evidence for this? Again, we need something to go on, tracks of such a creature, screams for help, signs of a struggle, something to back up such an explanation. There seems to be little of this.

So if it's not Bigfoot, serial killers, or wild animals accounting for many of these disappearances, what's left? Well, in some cases, people have seen strange lights or objects in the sky when these things occur and they have reported them. Therefore, we have some evidence for this idea, at least. If so, then the more likely answer would seem to be such disappearances are somehow connected to UFOs.

In addition, when we have over one million people in this country alone who claim to have been abducted by UFOs, is it then such a far-fetched idea to think some people may be abducted permanently and in isolated places, such as our national parks? Remember, many UFO sightings and encounters do seem to occur in highly isolated regions or in the dead of night in some rural locale.

Therefore, it might be reasonable to conclude UFOs are the culprits in these disappearances in our national parks, as well. For me, the probability is highest that UFOs are responsible for people vanishing and I say this not because I simply favor such a viewpoint, but because it comes down to a simple process of elimination. This seems the most likely probability. The available evidence would seem to indicate this as the most probably cause.

As always, this conclusion is based on the available evidence to date. Should that evidence change, I would then reconsider the likelihood of UFOs being the cause. To date, no such contrary evidence in any real amount seems to exist. At least, there isn't enough, a sufficient quantity to alter this conclusion for me.

If people kept reporting strange Bigfoot tracks, or if matted hair of an unknown beast appears tangled in twigs or branches at these locations, then I might consider the idea of a Bigfoot as being the true cause of the vanishings. Yet, as we've described earlier in this book, some of the disappearance don't occur where a Bigfoot could possibly be (the constantly busy Holland or Lincoln Tunnel, for instance, or on board a bus?). So I just don't think this is the cause, or at least, certainly not the only one.

Of course, the question then looms large in one's mind as to why. Why are so many people abducted, just to be returned? Why are others taken for good? I will visit this question again later in this book, but for now let's move on. Next, I would like to discuss the fact that people disappear in groups, and not just as isolated individuals.

CHAPTER 16—DISAPPEARANCE OF GROUPS OF PEOPLE

"I believe that these extraterrestrial vehicles and their crews are visiting this planet from other planets—which obviously are a little more technically advanced than we are here on earth".
—**Astronaut L. Gordon Cooper**

At this point, we have only discussed the disappearance of individuals. As I have shown, some people have vanished under stranger circumstances than others have. Nevertheless, let me reiterate here, as well, that most people disappear for a variety of reasons one would consider as "normal." By normal, I mean they can be accounted for with the usual answers, and not include any stranger solutions to those disappearances.

Therefore, although hundreds of thousands of people disappear each year, most surface again. At the very least, we can ascertain their whereabouts. Then there are those other individuals who vanish without a trace.

Under the chapter on Forbidden Zones, I've mentioned the vile vortices. Again, these are areas where people disappear. Sometimes, they vanish in groups, while traveling in planes or aboard ships, etc. Therefore, it is already a well-established fact many people have vanished in large groups under strange circumstances. However, some have also disappeared in groups outside of such enigmatic regions. Therefore, we can't neatly confine the problem just to the vile vortices. Groups of people disappear on a regular basis elsewhere, as well. Cases in point:

Flannan Isles Lighthouse, December 1900. This is a strange story. What's more, it is an enduring mystery. The lighthouse, on a rocky island near the coast of Scotland, had three men at one time stationed there as a normal matter. They kept the light lit for safety reasons, of course.

Then, a passing steamer noticed the light was out and so reported this when it came to its next port of call. At the time, there wasn't much concern about this. After all, the lighthouse keepers might have been experiencing a temporary difficulty with the light. Besides, there were three of them. If one or two were sick, this would still leave the third man to fix the problem. In any case, there would soon be a relief keeper force sent out, along with others who would bring provisions to the lighthouse. This was standard procedure.

When the appointed time came just days later, such a relief group did go. Once reaching the lighthouse, though, they met with a mystery. Upon entering the grounds, they found the gate to the lighthouse closed, as it should have been. The same held true for the door of the lighthouse proper.

They inspected the interior of the building. There was an overturned kitchen chair. Beds were unmade. The clock had stopped for want of winding. Other than this, nothing seemed out of the ordinary. The relief group searched the entire small rock of an island. Of the men, they found nothing. Two of the oilskin coats, which protected the men from wet weather, were missing from their normal place of storage. This indicated two of them had suited up in them. However, a third set of oilskins was still there. This meant one of the men had foregone the use of them and implied two staffers had gone out without the third one.

This was all the searchers found. Of the lighthouse crew, nothing was ever seen again. They had all simply vanished forever. No tools or implements had been left lying anywhere on the island to indicate from where they might have disappeared.

Various explanations were proffered. Some thought one might have murdered the other two and then committed suicide. However, there was no evidence for such a thing at all. There had been no sign of any violence whatsoever, except, possibly, for the one overturned chair. Still, to kill the men so suddenly would seem to have meant using some type of weapon in order to do the job quickly, such as a knife, hammer, or other such implement.

Yet, there was no blood found anywhere. There was no sign of any weapon that might have been used left lying about the place. The log of the lighthouse did not mention anything in the way of personality conflicts among the men, anything about any sort of divisions developing between them. Moreover, since the last entry in the log showed they knew they were close to the time of being relieved, why would one kill any of the others? All a potential murderer would have to do would be to control himself for a while, wait just a few more days, and he would be off the island for good. Murder simply wasn't necessary under the circumstances.

No, the idea of a murder/suicide did not seem reasonable, given the available evidence, or lack of it. The Northern Lighthouse Board concluded the same thing. The log had mentioned some damage, but a prior storm had caused this. There was no record of a storm in the time they were there. At least, nothing of any significance, for there was nothing stated in the log about such an event.

The Board concluded drowning had been the reason for the disappearances. They felt two of the men had been washed away by an unusually large wave. They thought perhaps the third man remaining in the lighthouse, had looked out and seen this, or perhaps the wave coming. He had then rushed out to help them, but had then drowned, as well, either in the initial wave, or a subsequent one that followed close after the first.

Yes, there are rogue waves, and sometimes quite large ones. They do exist. However, the area where the men worked was well above sea level. In fact, it was so high; the idea of a rogue wave reaching to such a height seems extremely unlikely. What's more, the third man would not have gone so far down as to be with the other two, but rather, would have called to them from higher up to start climbing higher to safer ground. This would have been far quicker to do to warn them, then laboriously climbing down to where they were, only to have to ascend once more to escape the wave. Lack of time due to the approaching wave would have demanded he do this, call down to them as quickly as he could. Yet, he, too, had vanished. So did he climb down? If so, why?

Was there then a second rogue wave, one even higher than the first to wash him away? Again, if so, wouldn't he have seen such a wave coming, also? If the first rogue wave was unlikely to reach such a height, how could the second one have gone even higher? Besides, seeing it coming (as he might have the first), wouldn't the keeper have fled back in the direction of the lighthouse and the safety it afforded?

Furthermore, apparently he took the time to lock the lighthouse door, as well as the gate on his way out, so the suggestion he was in a rush to save lives from an incoming rogue wave racing toward that little island does not seem to have much merit in any case.

No, the idea of a rogue wave, or two of them, causing the three just to disappear seems an unlikely proposition at best. So what did cause all three men to vanish under such mysterious circumstances? The answer is, nobody seems to know. They simply vanished forever.

USS Cyclops, February 1918. The USS Cyclops, an American Navy ship, had departed from Rio de Janeiro, Brazil. The ship made one unscheduled stop in Barbados. It then sailed homeward, traveling to Baltimore, Maryland. It never made it. The ship vanished. No one has seen any sign of it ever again.

The inevitable rumors began, as they always do in such cases. The ship had carried a large cargo of manganese, which under the right conditions, can be highly flammable and therefore, explosive. Some suggested carrying so much cargo, and having endured a storm, perhaps the vessel simply sank. Yet, no radio communications from the ship ever told of any trouble. If this happened, it happened very swiftly, indeed.

Others suggested the ship might have been a victim of a German submarine. Some suggested that the captain, who was German born, had taken the vessel to the Germans. Yet, there is no record in the German archives of such a ship having ever come to them, or of any submarine torpedoing the craft. Besides which, the crew vanished along with the ship. This means that unless the Germans committed mass murder of the crew to get a rather mundane US Naval cargo ship, this theory seems to be unlikely.

The U.S. Navy seems to have arrived at the same conclusion, for they discounted all such ideas. At the end of their formal investigation, they said, *"Many theories have been advanced but none that satisfactorily accounts for her disappearance."* In short, the U.S. Navy concluded the disappearance of the USS Cyclops was a total mystery and one without any viable explanation to provide a satisfactory cause, let alone an answer.

Peter Fawcett, May, 1925. I classify this under the group section of people who have disappeared because more than just one person disappeared. Peter Fawcett, a British archaeologist, one who was famous in the early 1900s, set out on an expedition into the interior of South America. Jack, his son, went along with them.

On May 25, 1925, Fawcett telegraphed home to let his wife know that he, along with his son, and another fellow by the name of Raleigh Rimmell, set out to explore an unknown region of the South American jungle. Peter Fawcett was intent on finding a lost city, a legendary one, which he referred to simply as "Z."

As a brief side note, this example involves a rather weird synchronicity for me. I'd never heard of Peter Fawcett or this expedition, not ever. While researching for this book, I came across this incident and felt it was right to include it here. That very same evening, I had run a search on Benedict Cumberbatch, an up-and-coming actor of the last few years. Under the information listed for him was the fact he is to be in a new movie, and the film is all about Peter Fawcett and his trip into the South American jungles!

The article said this movie will debut this year (2015). Again, I'd never even heard of Peter Fawcett. I knew nothing about him, but then on the same day, I not only learned of his existence, but then later that a film was coming out about him, and through two totally and seemingly unconnected events. There are those who say there are no such things as coincidences. I'm beginning to believe that just might be true because of this particular synchronicity.

In any case, in the real life version, this was the last that anyone ever heard of Peter Fawcett or his fellow travelers, including his son. They simply vanished without a trace. They never recovered any remains. No one found any of their equipment, either.

Of course, just as with all the other cases, rumors and theories quickly took root. Some thought native tribesmen killed the men. Others thought they died in some terrible accident. Yet, there is no evidence for any of this. No rumors, stories, or legends of their murder or any such thing have ever been uncovered.

Yes, many of the local tribes were hostile, but this had not changed from Fawcett's first visit to the region. It wasn't as if they hadn't been prepared for such an eventuality and had failed to take precautions. After the better part of the century, something should have surfaced, but nothing has.

A further note; despite Fawcett's own wishes as stated before he embarked on his sojourn, many people tried to find them. Over the years that followed, many such attempts were made. These resulted in the deaths of over 100 people! Yet oddly, and unlike Fawcett and his group, all those deaths have been accounted for.

This is just as one would expect; that ultimately the truth would out. However, in the case of Fawcett, his son, and their fellow traveler, Raleigh, this has never happened. So why are these hundred would-be rescuers' deaths explained, but not the three men who caused such missions to set out in the first place? Again, it is a mystery and one to which we might never get an answer.

I could go on with many other accounts of groups of people disappearing, but I feel enough has been said about the Bermuda Triangle, the Dragons Triangle, and such places, in other books, as well as on television. So to continue in this vein would be overkill. With so many people having been recorded as having disappeared in groups, as well, as individuals, I just don't think I need to belabor the point by mentioning more of these examples.

There are few of us these days who are not aware of the many ships and planes that have disappeared in such regions, along with all their crewmembers and passengers under mysterious circumstances. This is with no sign or trace of them or their vessels ever seen again. This brings us to a possible final example for this chapter.

Malaysia Airlines Flight 370, March 2014. Are there events like this occurring in the present day, mass disappearances? Yes, unfortunately, there are. Disappearances continue to happen all the time. Few of us, for example, are unaware of the ill-fated flight of Malaysia Airlines Flight 370. The jet, along with 239 crew and passengers vanished while on a flight from Kuala Lumpur, Malaysia, to Beijing China. This occurred on March 8, 2014.

The plane simply seems to have vanished. Searchers are unable to find any trace of it and it now has been over a year. There's been no sign of any wreckage or debris washing up on any shore, and despite an incredibly extensive search for the plane, and/or any remains of passengers or debris of the jet, not a single clue as yet been discovered as to its fate. Since then, another plane has gone down just south of the Dragon's Triangle and unlike the ill-fated Flight 370, they found the debris and dead in short order, in a matter of just a couple of weeks. This didn't happen with Flight 370.

I personally hope that something is found that would explain the disappearance of Flight 370. Still, after so much time, one begins to wonder if this will be just another mysterious disappearance of a large group of people that is never solved. I hope not. I hope it falls into the category of the 95 percent of cases that are explainable. Otherwise, this means that for relatives and friends of those who vanished onboard the Malaysian aircraft, closure might never take place. This would be a sad and lamentable thing to have as a result.

CHAPTER 17—DISAPPEARANCE OF VILLAGES AND MORE

"Flying saucers are real. Too many good men have seen them, that don't have hallucinations."
—Captain Edward 'Eddie' Rickenbacker

Many people don't realize that it isn't just individuals who disappear or groups of people, those on airplanes or ships that disappear, as well, but entire populations of communities vanish, too. This is not a new phenomenon. It, too, has been going on for a very long time and so is profound in its implications. Even the United States is not immune. In the earliest days of colonization of North America, a colony vanished.

Most of us in America know at least the rudiments of the story of Virginia Dare, her disappearance and that of the ill-fated colony she belonged to on Roanoke Island, Virginia, but since it is so strange, I added it here for those around the world who may not be aware of the more pertinent details of the tale.

Virginia Dare (exact date of death still a mystery (1587-1590?), was born in August 1587 in North America, in the English colony situated on Roanoke Island, Virginia (at the time—now the island is under North Carolina jurisdiction). Her parents were Ananias and Eleanor Dare. Virginia Dare was born August 18, 1587.

Her birth is significant for two reasons. First, she was the first child to be born in the colony, and for that matter, in the New World. In addition, her mother, Eleanor, was the daughter of the governor, John White, of the colony.

That same year, 1587, John White returned to England, for the colony was in need of more supplies. Three years would pass before his return. When he did arrive at the colony in August of 1590, he found all the inhabitants had vanished. The buildings had been collapsed, seemingly on purpose, and as John White wrote: *"the houses [were] taken downe."*

This told him and his companions the site had been deserted for some time already. There was no sign of any violence or other cause for this abandoning of the colony that they could ascertain. The colonists had all simply disappeared, all 17 women, 11 children, and 80 men had gone for good. Nobody ever saw any of them again.

This time, however, it was not quite without any trace at all. Found carved into one of the fort's posts was the single word: "Croatoan." In addition, the letters "Cro" had been carved into a tree, as well. No one has any idea what this message meant.

Moreover, an even stranger part of all this was the colonists seemed to have taken down the buildings in an orderly fashion, suggesting there had been no panic or sudden cause for flight to some presumed safer place or refuge. In other words, the abandonment of the settlement by all these people appears to have been orderly. The question is why?

Furthermore, this disappearance doesn't seem to have been a forced one. Again, there was no sign of violence having happened, no evidence of any battle, no remains of colonists found. To add credence to this idea of a lack of any problem with the natives or anyone else, for that matter, was that John White had arranged for a coded message in the event of any trouble. He had ordered the colonists to carve a cross into a tree close to the settlement, in the shape of a Maltese Cross, if they had been forced to leave the site for any reason. They didn't find any such cross, which by the way, would have been much quicker and easier to carve than "Croatoan."

However, John White took the word "Croatoan" to mean Croatoan Island, which has since been renamed Hatteras Island. However, he was in no position at the time to mount any sort of a search there. Thus, the fate of the colonists, of the "Lost Colony" as it has come to be called, is still a mystery, even to this day.

Various claims by a few Native Americans did result. For instance, one report said the colonists had been attacked and the remaining survivors had fled to the safety of the Chesapeake Indian tribe. Another claim by Chief Powhatan was his people had mounted a surprise attack and murdered the colonists. He even displayed some evidence for this idea in the form of a piece of a musket, the barrel, as well as a mortar and pestle.

Still, these stories seem highly unlikely to be true. First, the deliberate and systematic dismantling of the buildings in the colony suggests no such sudden attack took place. Furthermore, no signs of any sort of battle have ever been discovered, also seeming to give the lie to such accounts.

Croatoan Island did have a tribe friendly to the settlers, so the idea they might have gone there is certainly not impossible. There were even later reports of natives with "gray eyes" to give credence to the idea the colonists had settled there and ultimately interbred with the Native Americans.

However, this, too, seems not to have any real evidence to support this idea. The colonists were supposed to carve their destination in the tree along with the Maltese Cross. They did not do this—no Maltese Cross. Still, they must have had time, considering the effort and need to tear "*downe*" the houses of their settlement required such time.

Therefore, why not leave a full message? Moreover, the rescuers found no graves containing the remains of any of the settlers, either at the site of the original colony, or on Croatoan Island. Furthermore, that island was hardly so far away that some of the colonists couldn't have returned to Roanoke Island later to check for help from the returning governor.

Finally, evidence of natives with gray eyes seems not to exist in the present day, and even if it did, it still wouldn't account for the fact many of the colonists had blue eyes and there has been no sign of this in the indigenous people of the area, either.

Still, with the number of colonists involved, and no bodies found, one would have to presume all or most would have made it to the nearby island, if this was their intended target. This being so, there should be much more genetic evidence for them having made it there and interbred with the natives. There seems to be no real evidence for this so far.

Later in the 1930's, a series of carved stones were discovered. These so-called "Eleanor Dare Stones" told a story of a flight to safety, of the death of her husband, etc., and ultimately, the death of Virginia Dare years later when the colony had found a new home in the wilderness far from the original colony. These stones were later proved a hoax.

To this day, and despite continuing rumors of sightings of various members of the colony having lived or been held captive amongst the native tribes of the time (all hearsay and none verified), nobody seems to have any idea what happened to Virginia Dare or the Lost Colony. They simply seem to have vanished from the face of the Earth...again. Moreover, they seem to have done it in an orderly way.

Angikuni Village, Canada, November 1930. Now we come to an even more curious case, and that is a native village situated on the edge of Angikuni Lake. This lake is actually an estuary formed by the Kazan River and lies in one of the more remote regions of Canada, a region known as Kivalliq in the Nunavut area. It is here that an entire village of people vanished.

The problem with this story is there are multiple versions, ones added to over time. This is a common problem with such events. Tales grow with the retelling over the years. Numbers become inflated. Worse, newspapers at the time this occurred had no problem using photographs from other sites, as if they were pictures of the actual site in question. Even as late as the 1940s and 1950s, movie newsreels did this, restaging events, and then showing them as if they had just happened and had been filmed at the time the incident had occurred.

Therefore, to arrive at the truth of something in such cases is not easy. Thus, it is with this tale. However, after extensive research, there does seem to be real validity to the story. Just what is the story? Well, Joe LaBelle, a fur trapper, sought shelter, and so journeyed to the village in question. However, he found the place deserted. None of the 25 to 30 people was there.

It did look as if they had deserted the place not long before, but it also looked as if they had fled the village without taking anything of value with them. This included those things they'd need for survival, such as food, extra clothing, guns, etc.

Furthermore, they hadn't departed by way of the boats down on the "lake." These *"wave-battered"* boats were still there, unused.

Despite his attempting to locate anyone over the next few hours, all of Joe Labelle's efforts were in vain. There was no one, not in the village, or anywhere nearby. This presented a real problem for him. Why would the native Inuit people leave their domiciles in below-freezing weather, and without taking any of the necessities for survival with them? Why would they leave at all? Where did they go?

So shaken was Labelle, that despite his exhaustion, he decided not to stay. Instead, he traveled a long distance under terrible weather conditions to the nearest place he could send a telegraph to the authorities. He sent his telegram to the RCMP, or Royal Canadian Mounted Police. When they arrived, he told him his story of the deserted village.

Here, the story starts to get on less firm ground. According to several sources, such as the book, *The World's Great UFO Mysteries* by authors Nigel Blundell and Roger Boar, the Mounties paused in their journey at a hut. They told the residents there that they were on their way to Lake Angikuni because of a reported problem there.

When asked if their hosts had heard or seen anything unusual, they said they had spotted something strange flying several days before. They claimed the object changed its appearance, converting into a more bullet-shaped one, and so transforming from a cylinder-shape in the process. The book also claimed the number of disappeared to be much larger than the first number stated, being as many as possibly 2,000 people.

The books also claimed the Mounties later saw blue lights flitting about the sky, and that these lights were definitely not part of the Aurora Borealis, the Northern Lights. However, this is also from later reports, and so cannot be verified as being part of the original account. Later reports claimed there were open graves, the bodies having been removed, which would be very odd, indeed, since the Inuit people consider such burials sacred and not to be tampered with ever. Furthermore, the frozen ground would have been impossible to dig, so how were the graves excavated if this was so? Yet another account tells of the gravestones of the dead being stacked in either one or two neat piles.

In addition, there was an account that some dogs, tied to a leash, had starved to death, although from the look of things at the time, the villagers hadn't long departed the area. So how could the dogs die of starvation so quickly in such a short timespan?

There are even more such weird accounts about the disappearing village, but again, I've decided to forgo these in the interests of trying to remain as close as possible to the original account. The reason for mentioning some of the above is simply that these are cited in more than one book, and so may have actually occurred.

However, personally, and not finding corroborative evidence from the original account, as published in the **Le Pas Manitoba** newspaper, by reporter Emmet E. Kelleher, again, I felt the later details might be in question. The original article, the one published on November 28, 1930, being much closer to the time of the actual event, for me would tend to have more truth to it and less embellishment than much later and possibly therefore more embroidered accounts.

Unfortunately, the publishing of an old photo from another Inuit site didn't lend extra credence to his account of the whole affair, either. Do remember, though, this was the norm for newspapers of the time. When the reporters didn't have any current photos of something, it was a common thing done then, and even much later, as mentioned by such things being done with our own newsreels from the 1940s and 1950s. In other words, doing such a thing wasn't a sign of a hoax, because using substitute photos was nothing out of the ordinary, but rather an accepted practice at the time for the media of the day.

Some say the first account wasn't in the **Le Pas Manitoba** paper, but in the **Danville Bee**, but this is a moot point now. That the **Le Pas Manitoba** account of the disappearing villagers was one of the earliest, if not the earliest, is generally accepted.

The story came to prominence in 1937 again, when the much more detailed versions of it appeared in print. Decades later, in 1959, in his book, *The Vanishing Village of Angikuni* by Frank Edwards, the author reiterates and retells these 1937 accounts, as do Roger Boar and Nigel Blundell in their later book, *The World's Greatest UFO Mysteries*, (1982-1991). The accounts grew in size and detail.

In the 1980's, the Royal Canadian Mounted Police claimed the whole affair had been created for Frank Edward's book. They further claimed no such event had ever occurred, that they had no record of such a thing happening. They said:

"The story about the disappearance in the 1930's of an Inuit village near Lake Angikuni is not true. An American author by the name of Frank Edwards is purported to have started this story in his book Stranger than Science. *It has become a popular piece of journalism, repeatedly published and referred to in books and magazines. There is no evidence however to support such a story. A village with such a large population would not have existed in such a remote area of the Northwest Territories (62 degrees north and 100 degrees west, about 100 km west of Eskimo Point). Furthermore, the Mounted Police who patrolled the area*

recorded no untoward events of any kind and neither did local trappers or missionaries."

So what is the truth? Certainly, Edward Boar and Blundell's claims of how many disappeared seem to be grossly inflated. The Mounties are right—a village of such a large size would have definitely been on maps, and any such event would have made world headlines at the time. So such a large number of disappeared seems unlikely. This is why I've gone with the original newspaper account, which did exist, and which claimed the number was closer to 25 to 30 people, which seems much more in line with reality.

However, the RCMP's claim the event never took place and the village never existed does seem to be incorrect, as well. After all, Frank Edward didn't publish his account until 1959, but the first account(s) were the newspaper article(s) published in the same year as the Lake Angikuni disappearances took place, almost 30 years prior to Frank Edward's book. Were Canada's own newspapers of the time creating stories out of thin air? This, too, seems unlikely.

As it turns out, Joe Labelle was a real person, although the Mounties claim there is no evidence he ever trapped in that area. Yet, such lack of evidence of where trappers trapped was hardly readily available or recorded as a regular thing. First, fur trappers were often non-communicative about where they trapped. Such locations were often highly prized secrets.

This was especially so if the trapping were good there, for fear that if their locations were found, other trappers would move in and "horn in on their territory."

Secondly, trappers hardly ever made public logs of where they trapped for strangers' accessibility. Fur trappers, it seems, are not ones for keeping journals of their travels. Moreover, they could be gone for long periods and so range over wide areas, often spending whole seasons in the wilderness, traveling sometimes at random. Therefore, the idea the Mounties had no record of Joe Labelle trapping in the Angikuni area means practically nothing. More likely, the surprise would have been if they did have such a record.

Likewise, it seems there was more than one investigation into the matter by the RCMP. Besides the one that occurred at the time of the event, on January 17, 1931, a Sergeant J. Nelson initiated another one. He later claimed there was no basis in fact for the story.

However, authors Geoff Dittman and Chris Rutkowski, in their book, *The Canadian Report: The Best Cases Revealed*, claimed that Nelso based his findings on just one short conversation with the owner of a trading post, a person who claimed he'd heard nothing about such an event as the disappearance at Lake Angikuni from other travelers. This hardly seems grounds for discounting the event as never having happened, based on just one person's negative testimony, and furthermore, hardly qualifies as a "diligent" investigation on Nelso's part.

As with all such controversial cases, skeptics, as well as adherents, seem to come out of everywhere, intent on either proving or disproving the event took place. In other words, they have "axes to grind." Therefore, neither group is unbiased in their approach.

For instance, some skeptics point to the claim the villagers' boats were battered by the waves on the lake, according to the original story. They claim that in November, the lake would have been frozen over. Yet, the lake wasn't really a lake, but rather more of an estuary, and so the water isn't necessarily entirely fresh by any means, but rather could well be brackish, containing salt, which would keep it from freezing over in

November temperatures as a normal freshwater lake might do. Only later, closer to, or even in the dead of winter, would such a thing be likely to happen.

Furthermore, there were published newspaper accounts at the time of the disappearing villagers, so someone had to have reported something on the matter, or why would such reports appear in the papers at that particular time? It would seem given this, certain facts do seem to be true:

1. Joe Labelle existed.

2. He was a fur trapper.

3. There was at least one newspaper account for sure, but more likely two, about villagers disappearing in the Lake Angikuni area.

4. Although the numbers of disappeared seem to have been inflated in later versions, the more reliable estimate is 25 to 30 people actually disappearing.

5. As to later versions of the account, including the idea of an object seen in the skies, and/or strange blue lights flitting around, this is less verifiable. Yet, reports of UFO sightings were rare in those days, so to have something said like this, in itself, might mean the reports are true.

Disappearance of Chinese Village, October 2010. Reports of villagers disappearing came from China in 2010. The event occurred on October 10. The location of the occurrence was in the Shaanxi Province, in the foothills of the Qinling Mountains. This means the incident did not take place very far from a nuclear facility there. This fact was to raise some questions about the reason for the disappearing villagers later on. Besides journalists who independently reported about this event, a report was also published on Yahoo News.

The article says that all the inhabitants of a nearby village (the reporter was situated in the next village over from there), "*disappeared overnight.*" Nobody knows, or seems to know what happened to them. They simply seemed to have vanished, apparently for good. The news quickly gained high Internet status, and then was repeated around the world.

An official radio report initially spoke of the bizarre disappearance. It said that at 10 o'clock in the evening on October 10, inhabitants of the nearby town of Xian Yang witnessed odd glowing objects in the night sky, and the objects appeared to be rotating. However, the light coming from them was diffuse, and therefore, no ready source was ascertainable. Furthermore, the report added that the witnesses, while viewing the objects in the sky, said they felt "*strange.*" This display of lights went on for over two hours according to the same report.

There is more to this story, but we're not concerned with the details here, but rather the main points of the event. One thing should be mentioned, however, and this is the fact there was a spotlight in the main square of the town. However, witnesses say that this had already been turned off and had been extinguished before the weird lights began crisscrossing the heavens.

Sometime during the next hours, or perhaps day, reports came of the abandoned village. Nobody was to be found there. Furthermore, there were reports of troops along the main highway in the region. They had closed the throughways. Troop movements were noticed. These included tanks, armored personnel carriers, soldiers, and what looked like mobile missile and/or rocket launchers. The report also said the military and/or authorities cordoned off the area. No one was allowed entry.

The Chinese government, through official media outlets, later stated that all these were just rumors and to their knowledge, nothing out of the ordinary had taken place at all. This fueled the skeptics, and they then called the whole thing a hoax, or a mere rumor that had gotten out of control on the Internet. This is not out of the norm for skeptics. Rather than investigating the facts, they more often than not must immediately shout: "HOAX!" This is often whether they have any evidence for it being so, or not.

The odd part of this is that skeptics would take the official word of the Chinese government, when it is one notorious for putting spin on events any time it wants to, and then the skeptics utilizing that as a basis for their dismissal of the event? The Chinese government is more than well known for controlling its news media. That Communist government doesn't hesitate to ban stories, to force journalists to alter their stories and the facts related to them, or even to make events into non-events by sealing off access to certain areas.

As a case in point, this is currently true for a region in the northwest of China, at Ürümqi, the capital of the Province of Xinjiang, where they have an ongoing issue with Muslim Uighur separatists. Access is highly restricted. Foreign and Chinese journalists alike, are kept under constant surveillance, watched, and interfered with if they try to speak to any citizens there. Their cameras are frequently confiscated and stripped of their contents. Foreign reporters have to smuggle out any video they have.

So again, why would skeptics quote the Chinese government as a reliable source that nothing had happened with regard to disappearing villagers, when that government has an incredible record of being so unreliable with regard to the facts of just about anything? A more unreliable source for the skeptics would be hard to find. Then, this is part of the almost schizophrenic-like approach some skeptics have to any such phenomena, Some of them will seize on anything that justifies them denigrating or refusing to believe something happened.

However, there are some serious problems with this contention of nothing having happened, besides the unreliability of the Chinese government's statements. First, the radio station that had first announced the news was an officially government-sanctioned one. Therefore, *de facto*, the Chinese government had, through the auspices of its own radio station, gone on record to report the event as having actually occurred. Moreover, there is no reason to believe the official radio station was reporting a hoax at the time.

Secondly, the number of people who viewed the UFOs in the night sky in the nearby town was numerous. Furthermore, the display went on for hours, or as one reporter put it, *"a very long time."* Therefore, it's hard to countenance the idea the witnesses misinterpreted what they saw, since they had more than enough time to view the display in detail.

Third, if there had been some nuclear crisis or accident as an explanation for all this, one would expect government troops to move in, most certainly, and just as they did. One would also expect an attempt to suppress such news, since it would be extremely bad press. This, too, is a given.

However, besides the troops going there, we have to consider those reported armored personnel carriers and missile/rocket launchers, as well as tanks. Such equipment would be highly questionable as far as their practical use in the situation of a nuclear accident. Bringing missiles to the site of a nuclear accident is rather like "bringing coals to Newcastle."

Skeptics also claim the lights in the sky were the spotlights. This, too, would seem very unlikely. The local inhabitants would have often seen the spotlights, nightly, and on cloudy nights, as well as on clear ones. They would certainly know the difference between those spotlights reflecting off any such clouds versus the blue lights (as also reported in the Angikuni Village Incident).

Again, as is usual, skeptics never credit the witnesses, longtime residents, and used to such things as those spotlights, with any ability to discern anything for themselves with reasonable accuracy. Yet, such skeptics, who weren't even there, often feel they have the answers. Answers they may have, but perhaps not the correct ones, because again, the spotlights had been turned off at their usual time, well before the display of blue lights started.

One other thing; the world was very quickly aware, via satellite photography, of the nuclear meltdown at Chernobyl in the then Soviet Union. We were also later able to verify with accuracy the amount of radiation released. No such evidence of any nuclear accident at the facility near the village of the disappeared has been discovered in this way. One can only assume then, that whatever happened, didn't involve a nuclear accident. So why the military going there?

One final thing with regard to this matter, as well; as we've shown earlier in this book, UFO sightings in and about the area of nuclear military sites and government military bases are common, both in the United States, and from all reports, in the former Soviet Union, too, as well as in many other countries. This is not a new phenomenon nor is it restricted to our country alone. Rather, this is a worldwide phenomenon. The fact UFOs appeared in such an area in China is hardly a surprise, then.

Just what happened to the disappearing villagers? Well, nobody seems to know, and as is usual with any government, when they don't want news released, it isn't released. What happened there on October 10 is a complete mystery. The fact that something very bizarre took place, though, does not seem to be a matter of doubt.

Yet another question about all this, besides the ultimate fate of those poor villagers, is why did the Chinese government so rapidly move in such a commanding force of firepower? Just what were they afraid of? Again, it may be a long time, if ever, before we find out. If that's the case, maybe we're lucky.

CONCLUSION

"I've been asked [about UFOs] and I've said publicly I thought they were somebody else, some other civilization."
—**Astronaut Eugene Cernan, Apollo 17, Los Angeles Times, 1973**

So how can we sum all this information up? What can we make of it all? We've discussed much about the whole UFO phenomenon, concentrating on its darker aspects, so what does this all mean?

Well, a quick recapitulation of just what has been discussed here might help to order things for us.

We've discussed the following topics in the first part of this book:

1. The idea there is a "Great UFO Conspiracy" being a fact and not just as a myth.

2. The idea that there actually does seem to be a great deal of evidence for a cover-up of this conspiracy.

3. We've discussed just how far our government might go, or some sort of shadow government might go, in order to keep the lid on this conspiracy.

4. We've described just what the government definition of UFOs is.

In the second part of this book, I then moved on to the following topics:

1. Damages and injuries caused by UFO encounters.

2. Civilians killed by UFO encounters.

3. Military deaths involved with UFO encounters.

4. That most puzzling and frightening subject, the deaths of many researchers who investigated UFOs.

In Part three, I discussed the idea that;

1. Certain areas of the Earth seemed to be "forbidden to us," and not only here on our planet, but perhaps on the Moon, as well.

2. Abductions of innocent people.

3. Crop circles.

4. Animal mutilations.

In the final part of this book, I focused on:

1. The disappearance of individuals.

2. The disappearance of groups of people.

3. The apparent disappearance of entire populations of people from villages.

So again, what can we make of all of this? Well, we can start by drawing some general conclusions based on all this evidence.

First, since the sightings of UFOs are in such huge numbers, if one only takes the government-supplied idea that about 5% of sightings can't be explained by any conventional means, then we come up with that figure of over 50,000 unexplained sightings of UFOs, worldwide, each year. This means no normal solutions can explain them away and the number of such unexplained sightings is incredible. One might even say formidable.

Second, from this, I can reasonably argue that UFOs do exist, that they are here, and they seem to be everywhere on our Earth and perhaps on our Moon, as well (based on evidence in my other books).

Third, given the huge amount of testimony by so many former employees of NASA, astronauts, people who have worked for the government, military personnel (often with security clearances), and so many others, as opposed to the government's official stance against it all, I have to also conclude there seems to be some type of cover-up going on.

Fourth, because of the size and scope of the cover-up, it would seem that it must be our government doing it. Whether this is in the form of a shadow government, our regular government, both, and/or the participation in some way of extraterrestrials, as well, is harder to say. Nevertheless, that there is an ongoing cover-up does seem to be a fact.

Furthermore, given the available evidence, it would seem that some form of shadow government is involved. As to just how "shadowy" that government might be, meaning in other words, how little the regular government may be aware of it is also hard to say.

Our military-industrial complex has long been involved in black projects, projects whose funding is derived by clandestine and circuitous means, so as not to allow the general public, and/or Congress (at least, most members of it) to be aware of such projects. They have done this for decades.

We all know this is a fact, as mentioned with the Stealth Bomber and Stealth Fighter programs, etc. One has to assume it has involved other projects, as well, including those having to do with UFOs, and such hidden places as Area 51. Remember, this is an area the government even denied existed until recent years, and despite the whole world knowing of it. Therefore, our government will attempt to cover up things even when it would appear pointless to do so.

Now I come to the nature of this cover-up/conspiracy, as discussed in the book and the question of just how far those who wish to keep a lid on the whole thing, would go. However, I also have to ask why they would go so far, if indeed they are doing this. If they are going to extremes, even arranging for "accidents" for researchers, journalists, and investigators, and/or "assisted" suicides, one has to wonder what is so vital, so important, that it is worth killing these people to keep it secret?

We know there have been many deaths of such people. We know these deaths seem to have started with Secretary Forrestal in 1949. We also know he is supposed to have been a member, one of the few civilian members of the secretive group that many believe exists, known as MJ (or MAJESTIC) 12. We also know that this seemingly highly rational and well-respected man died under mysterious circumstances. Even the hospital where he died has had staff members say words to this effect.

Nor is Secretary Forrestal alone in this type of demise. I've included in the book a lengthy list of people involved someway or somehow in the UFO phenomenon that have died in mysterious circumstances, through mysterious means, or simply disappeared altogether. Moreover, there also seems to be an unusually (statistically) high number of deaths due to different heart illnesses, strokes, and cancers (some very rare) for this group of people (researchers, scientists, journalists, UFO investigators), as opposed to the general population.

What does this mean? Well, it seems reasonable to conclude that not all of these deaths were "natural," not due to naturally occurring illnesses, and "natural" desires to commit suicide. Then, in addition, there are the deaths by outright murder. Overall, there have been some strange deaths, indeed.

For instance, murder of a scientist by so-called Satanists? Really? That stretches one's credulity to believe in such an explanation. Similarly, someone slipping off a bridge and into a river because they had a moment of dizziness? In addition, more than one dies this same way? Again, this stretches one's credulity. Because of course, the bridges had railings.

So it goes and continues to go. The sheer number of such deaths, by strange diseases, bizarre suicides, or murderers, is just hard to accept as something that occurs in the normal course of events. Is it possible? Yes, despite all the strangeness of some of these deaths, it is possible they occurred in the normal course of events.

However, is it probable? Statistically, this sort of thing is unlikely in the extreme. That such a group should be so targeted "naturally" by sheer chance, is just not very likely.

Let me put this more plainly. So convinced am I that some of these deaths are not "natural," that if someone pointed a gun at my head and said that my life depended upon the correct answer, I would have to say that some of those deaths were by design. I would have to admit that I believe they had been deliberately done for specific purpose, rather than just being a mere statistical aberration and normal, mundane events.

Why would I choose this answer? Because I honestly think, the response would ensure my continued existence under such a scenario. That's how sure I am of this. That's how certain I am this is correct.

One thing more and I have to say it clearly here; something is going on, and that something isn't good, judging by the nature of what it seems to involve.

Why do I say this? Well, the reasons seem self-evident to me, but I will go over them here. The fact people are being killed to apparently aid in this cover-up definitely does not bode well. The truth is, I, and some others, worry to varying degrees about even writing these sorts of books for this reason.

No, I don't think I'm in any great danger…yet, but yes, it is something fellow authors and I have had to consider to a greater or lesser extent, depending on the individual. Let me just add that to date, I have felt in no danger, had nothing odd happen, except, of course, for a couple of close-spaced incidents recently which are laughable.

On a recent radio interview, one that I did by phone, we were delayed starting by fifteen minutes. The phones at the place where they were conducting the interview had all suddenly gone out. So the host of the radio show had to use Skype to get through to me. Within minutes of the ending of the show, their phones came back on again. The host said this had *"never happened before."*

I joked, laughed it off, of course, and as one does under such circumstances, but even the host made a remark about the strangeness of that coincidence. As a result, he had asked me if I felt the government was "after" me, as well, during the course of the interview. He wanted to know if I had seen any signs of this. I told him I had not, at least not until the phone problem.

The second event took place a week later. I had recorded an interview for another radio show. Then, a week after this last event, I received an email. The embarrassed host said the interview had "disappeared." He was apologetic, and said he couldn't explain it, because they always made several backups of the interview, and stored them on more than one hard drive/computer. So how it could happen had him buffaloed. We had to repeat the entire interview for this reason.

Just strange coincidences? In all probability, yes, and I at least, think so, but again, there are those who say there are no such things as coincidences. If they're right, then what happened takes on a slightly scarier feel to it, a greater dimension of possibilities, and none of them would be good. But no, I'm not paranoid. I go about my daily business in no fear at all of my sudden and inexplicable demise.

That aside, I now come to the next step in our trying to figure all this out. If the UFO phenomenon is real, it definitely seems to be, and if there is a cover-up going on, a large-scale one that seems to resort to extreme measures to keep it so, then I next have to ask, why? Why would "they" go to such lengths, such extremes, and such expense to maintain such a massive cover-up effort? Well, let's consider a few things:

First, we know the majority of Americans now believe UFOs exist. Furthermore, almost as many feel the government is involved in a cover-up of the phenomenon. So for those who think our government (and other governments) are maintaining this cover-up just to protect us from panicking at the idea of such a thing being true, that UFOs actually exist, well, the cat is "already out of the bag," as the saying goes. Not only do most people know of UFOs, but again they believe they exist.

We should ask: why such a massive cover-up to hide something that is already believed as true by the majority of our citizens here in the US? Obviously, there is no panic going on, so the idea of it being a panic preventative just sounds like a hollow and rather specious argument at this point.

So what other reasons could there be to maintain such a widespread and sometimes deadly effort? Well, conspiracy theorists come up with several possibilities. These are:

1. The government has no control over the UFO phenomenon, is powerless to stop, control, or inhibit it, and is reluctant to admit it, because this might just cause a real panic. Therefore, by covering it up, there is no UFO phenomenon, so no need to admit to the government's inability to protect its citizens from them.

After all, to admit that some "others" have control of the skies that our skies are not "our" skies, and extraterrestrials occupy the high ground just might actually result in a real panic. If one fears that whether at home, on the road, or at work that they can be snatched, or have their children abducted and then be subjected to what amounts to torture would tend to destroy the average citizen's faith in their government.

Therefore, this might be a good reason to maintain a cover-up. Certainly, our society would change in many profound ways. At the very least, a "bunker mentality" might ensue. This would adversely affect our government's power and control of the situation, our individual lives, and our ability to function as a "normal" society.

2. The government and/or a shadow government might be in active collusion with extraterrestrials in maintaining the cover-up. Under this idea, we have two categories:

a. This could be that the government is powerless to stop the UFO/extraterrestrials and what they are doing with regard to abductions and/or disappearances. However, they have managed a tradeoff, an agreement, if you will. This would be where they keep it as secret as possible, downplay it every way they can, in exchange for the extraterrestrials also maintaining a clandestine approach to the whole thing.

In this way, the world could carry on with what most would consider a reasonably normal existence. We could continue to govern ourselves, so to speak. There would be a sort of *quid pro quo* established under this scheme, with the extraterrestrials getting what they want (us), and our government getting much of what it would desire, the continuation of daily existence for its citizens and itself pretty much as it always has been.

b. As if such a theory isn't scary enough, there is an even more frightening scenario and that is our government is in active collusion with extraterrestrials, aiding and abetting the cover-up because it's getting something it wants and so is willing to tradeoff the lives and wellbeing of its citizens in order to get this.

What do I mean by this idea? Well, many theorize the sudden and extreme rise in our technological capabilities, seeming to date back to just about the time of the Roswell Incident, might be evidence our government is getting help and information from extraterrestrials with regard to technological advances.

It took the entire time of recorded history to achieve the sum total of human knowledge we had by the early to mid-1950's. Since then, there has been an information and technological explosion, most of which seems, again, to date to just after the Roswell Incident. Let's take a quick look at some of these statistics:

—Based on figures supplied by the University of California, new information of the digital variety increased by 60 percent from 2003 to 2005. As a comparison better to understand this, this would be an increase of 57,000 times all the knowledge contained in the Library of Congress in that time. This is a phenomenal amount of new information! Moreover, the University of Berkeley believes that worldwide business information increases by at least 30% a year, again, a staggering amount.

—Information on the Internet doubles every six months and that time range is steadily dropping.

—Specifically, corporate information is doubling every six months, as well.

—Scientific knowledge is increasing to the point where it doubles every five years, and that time range is narrowing, too.

—Furthermore, our knowledge of biology also doubles every five years, with practical information of genetics doing so every 18 months to two years.

—Based on those same sources, technical knowledge doubles every three years and medical knowledge, overall, doubles every seven years.

—Finally, the sum total of human knowledge, which took from the beginning of recorded history to the 1950's, is now doubling at the rate of every two years, and this figure is shrinking fast. As it now stands, it is taking less than a year, some say just six months, to double. Again, even that number is shrinking quickly.

So how do we account for this massive explosion of knowledge in ever-shorter timespans? Again, some conspiracy theorists say it is because our government is receiving technological knowledge from an extraterrestrial species. I would be less inclined to entertain such a theory as fact, if it wasn't for the date that all this seemed to start, this information explosion we are currently undergoing. The coinciding with this all seeming to begin so soon after the Roswell Incident is, at the very least, troubling.

So if this is true, if our government is in collusion, and there certainly seems to be a fair amount of circumstantial evidence, at least, to support this contention, what does it mean for us as average citizens? Moreover, what does it mean for the extraterrestrials and us?

Well at this point, we have not only to consider the damages and injuries inflicted on us by various UFO encounters, but the deaths they cause us, as well. Some say these are incidental, not on purpose.

However, let's face facts here: if the UFOs didn't deliberately interfere with us in the first place, as they so often seem to do, then deaths and injuries wouldn't occur. We know they buzz our flying craft. We know they seem to seek out people at times. In addition, we know people have died under often mysterious and horrible circumstances. Furthermore, abductions seem to be rife, as well as animal mutilations and these are all worldwide. For those involved, it's obviously not a good thing. For the animals involved, it means their death.

Therefore, if nothing else, I would have to conclude the extraterrestrials, no matter who they are or what their origins, certainly don't appear to have our best interests at heart. This simply can't be, when people die in such numbers, become injured in even more numbers, and not just here, but again, around the world.

Then there is the disturbing matter of the permanent disappearances happening under mysterious circumstances. How else do we account for this? Did all these people, *en masse*, fly in planes, float on ships, or accidentally walk through gateways to other dimensions or times?

Alternatively, as seems more likely the case, did "something" or "someone" take them? Let's not forget all those reports of UFO sightings in the areas at the times some of these events took place. Well, logic would seem to dictate that all those sightings weren't just coincidences, but somehow are bound up in mysterious cause of all those disappearances.

Furthermore, either these people are falling into other dimensions in droves and quite by accident, or UFOs snatch them up. Since we have all those abductions where the victims claim extraterrestrials do just that, and since UFOs are seen in the skies when some disappearances occur (disappearance of the Chinese village, for example) it is more than reasonable to assume UFOs might be involved, might well be doing this. It would certainly seem the most obvious explanation, and an existing one, rather than reaching for something vaguer and more tenuous.

So what can we make of all this, all these negative interactions in so many UFO incidents? Well, the possible conclusions as to why this is happening, the possible reasons for it, are not good, not any of them, really. For instance, some UFO conspiracy theorists go so far to say that perhaps we are a food source for extraterrestrials, and this is why people disappear, get snatched by UFOs. Others say some of us are running experiments, and this is why they suffer repeated abductions. Still others say the extraterrestrials are in the midst of an attempt to create a hybridized species of humans, ones that might look like us, but have the soul of the aliens, so to speak, or at least their type of intelligence and mindset.

I find the humans-as-food idea hard to believe, myself, but I don't completely rule out the possibility, because I simply don't know. I wish I did. Moreover, perhaps I just don't want to believe this, because it is such a frightening and horrible idea. Still, which theory is the correct one, if any? Well, at present, we can't know for sure, but we can arrive at some logical conclusions about it all. These are:

1. Abductees in their millions (according to some estimates) do return to us.

2. The Disappeared, however and in their many numbers, never come back. We never see any of them again, as with Frederick Valentich and so many others.

3. Many incidents involving UFOs and USOs do involve damage, injuries, and even deaths.

This means UFOs, at least some of them, are not friendly to us. If this is so, then the occupants of such craft are not our "space brothers," as some contactees would have us believe. These people could well be the victims of extraterrestrial mental programming and/or propaganda disinformation to allay their fears.

There may be some benevolent extraterrestrials, but obviously, there must be at least one species that is not, given the evidence. Again, this has to be the conclusion, given the available evidence.

Why are they abducting people and then returning them? Well, again, we can logically come up with a number of reasons, at least, the mainstream ones:

1. The abductees are study cases, perhaps subjects of experiments, so the extraterrestrials can learn more about us as a species or those specific individuals.

2. They abductees are being altered somehow, as if the alien visitors were trying to change us genetically in some fashion—creating a hybrid race, for example.

3. The abductees are having tissue tests done and samples taken because the aliens need some of our genetic material, perhaps, as in to grow organs, or whatever. Some even claim it is to create an entirely new species, and that ultimately if not already, "we are they."

4. There is another idea, as well, and one which the host of Coast-To-Coast AM Radio, George Noory, and I discussed in my interview on the show. That is, perhaps the returned, the abductees, constitute a form of "sleeper cell," those who have been altered and programmed without their knowledge to act in a coordinated way under certain conditions, if triggered to do so. This may be a reason why so many report implants in their bodies.

These implants could be a form of programming device, meant to deliver commands to the subconscious of the abductees. Once accomplished, with these "programs" in place, the implants could then disintegrate, as they often seem to do, and then come out of the body on their own, as also seems to happen. This would be only after the "programming" was accomplished, already in place, perhaps permanently for those abductees/victims. In other words, maybe the abductees constitute a sleeping army, one ready to act on the extraterrestrials orders, should they be triggered to do so, again, rather like Soviet sleeper cells of spies did during the height of their Cold War with the West.

Yes, this is a frightening possibility. Nevertheless, it could be a real one. It would certainly explain why there are so many abductions, why they are "processed" as they are, and why so many of them have implants. Remember, the number of abductees estimated by some ufologists is in the millions! That would make for quite an "on-demand" army for extraterrestrials, if they wanted one.

The Disappeared. Now I come to the permanently disappeared and this is a hard topic for which to arrive at any reasonable conclusions, because we simply haven't any clues as to what happens to people after they permanently disappear. However, we do know that people have disappeared as individuals, in groups, sometimes large groups, and even entire populations of villages have vanished and that often, UFOs/extraterrestrials seem to be involved in some way. The question is why? Why would extraterrestrials do this? Why would they permanently abduct some, but not others?

Well, again, we have that "food source" idea that some conspiracy theorists truly believe in. However, again, I'm not so inclined to think this, because the logic of it simply isn't strong enough. Why then would UFOs mutilate animals, but not eat them? Why would they instigate crop circles?

Furthermore, why bother to hide the fact if we are their cattle fodder, so to speak? Surely, their technology is so far beyond ours that we could do nothing about it, even if we did all know? Then there is the question of why just the lone person vanishing here and there? This is hardly the most efficient way to harvest us as food, one would think.

Therefore, what other explanation could there be? Could it be as a source of slave labor, perhaps? This might be a real possibility, but then why take the handicapped, young children, and women? If they wanted us for hard physical labor, wouldn't they seek out the biggest, strongest, strapping men for the purpose? Why snatch a crippled old man off the front porch of his home?

The Disappeared seem to be almost random in their backgrounds, physicality, gender, and age. Therefore, just what is really going on with this matter?

The truth is, we don't know. It's hard even to come up with a convincing reason for the Disappeared. Still, it keeps happening, and worldwide, in numbers that are alarming. Why seize Frederick Valentich and his plane, for instance? Why steal a young woman walking on a trail in New England, or again, a crippled old man from his front porch? We just don't have the answers to that, because we can't fathom the purpose of such a thing.

However, again, we can try at least, to get closer to some truth or other. This might be an unpleasant truth, considering all the evidence, but then, that can't be helped. Why do I think this?

Well, first, we know something is happening and whatever it is, it is worth killing people over, it seems, to keep it quiet. Something is kept hidden by persons unknown, and this very probably could include our government and others, as well as even, perhaps, extraterrestrials. Again, whatever it is that's happening, seems to be worth killing over. That, in itself, is a terrifying idea.

Considering all this, and the behavior of so many UFOs with regard to hurting and killing our people in so many ways, we can only conclude that whatever is going on certainly may not be in our best interest. It sure isn't for those who have been the victims of all this.

In addition, logically, we then have to assume it isn't good for the Disappeared, as well. We have no reason to believe they would be treated any better, any more humanely, then anyone else in this regard. Therefore, whatever their ultimate fates might be, it's hard to think it is a good one.

For instance, are the Disappeared being taken to colonize another world and thus help ensure the survival of the human species? Not likely. One doesn't take the ill, old, and feeble to conquer a new world.

Perhaps the Disappeared are taken to educate and enlighten them as contactees think our "space brothers" might want? Again, not likely. Why bother to enlighten individuals if they are never going to be returned to us, integrated back into our society as the abductees are?

No, no matter how one looks at it, it's hard to come up with a convincing positive reason for these abductions. There simply doesn't seem to be any justification for a "happy ending" for them, as it were, and this is a terrible, unfortunate, and sad thing, and one, about which, we can't seem to do anything.

So when it comes to the question, *Quo Vadis*, "wither goest thou," for the Disappeared, we don't have a ready answer. What we can say is that wherever they have journeyed to, it is a permanent one, and it doesn't seem to be a good place to go.

My brother, was once asked a very pertinent question about what he felt about UFOs. The question was: "*Do you think humans are at the top of the food chain here on Earth?*" My brother had no ready reply to this, so he later asked me what I thought.

My answer, based on the available evidence to date, was; "*No, we are not at the top of the food chain. Certainly not. There are predators and there is prey, and it would seem to be, for whatever reasons, we are prey.*" It would seem we do not rule our skies and those that do are not compassionate creatures. They aren't bound by morals of any apparent sort familiar to us. They don't hesitate to do what they want, when they want, and how they want.

Is there any good we can get from all this? Well, we can only hope that not all the extraterrestrials are like this, amoral, or creatures without compassion, and that some do give a damn about us, because it seems we are helpless to stop what's going on, whatever that is. Worse, whatever is going on seems to have the hand of our government in it somehow, and not in a good way, either.

If you doubt this, if this idea of the extraterrestrials being a real and present danger to us is not to your liking, and you think the aliens "are our "space brothers" or "our friends," ones just here to help us, then consider this question:

Can anyone, anyone at all, anywhere, give an account of UFOs that have helped some of us in any real way whatsoever?

By this, I mean, some real and physical way, such as maybe they beamed someone out of a burning building, for instance? They seem to be able to do this well enough when it comes to abductions, after all. Have they led anyone lost, such as children in the woods, out of the forest by even so much as shining a beam of light for them to follow to safety? Have they warned anyone of deadly hurricanes, dangerous tsunamis, or anything like that at all?

The answer, of course, is "no." They have not. I can find no recorded instances of such a thing EVER having occurred. Yes, there are those who claim to have been mentally contacted and told stories such as the extraterrestrials are here to "elevate" us, or save us from ourselves, or whatever, but talk is cheap. Where, how, and when are they actually supposedly doing this? Are these contactees just poor dupes to make us think the extraterrestrials have our best interests at heart, which considering the garbled nature of some of these "messages," would seem to be an unlikely case?

Now I lay the challenge before you: Give me an instance where a UFO or its occupants did something besides buzzing our skies and aircraft (sometimes dangerously so), abducted people, damaged property, injured men, women, and children, mutilated animals, and/or abducted or disappeared people in their thousands?

Nor can we consider the rare abductee who say they were cured of a cancer or any such thing, while being abducted as positive evidence. First, we have no reliable data to support this claim. Secondly, the placebo effect is powerful, indeed, and so if they are told they were cured, they might well be cured (read Michael Talbot's *The Holographic Universe* for in-depth information on this phenomenon). This does not mean the extraterrestrials necessarily accomplished such a cure. Abductees often suffer from a condition that is close to, if not actually Post Traumatic Stress Disorder from what they underwent while abducted. Such information from them, what very little there is of it, would be highly suspect, therefore, and so must be considered as such.

Finally, if extraterrestrials actually have cured any abductees, perhaps it is to preserve these "subjects" because they are part of some ongoing experiment or hybridization program as many ufologists believe is happening. So in such a case, any such "miraculous cures" (if any) would not be for the benefit of us humans necessarily at all! I n any case, the evidence for such things happening is very minimal at best, and is far outweighed by the negatives, such as there being far more deaths than any potential or possible "cures." Ask one of the Disappeared how they feel about this idea? Oh yes, we can't, because they never come back...

In summation, this book has shown much evidence, a great deal of it, for the negative aspects of the whole UFO phenomenon, the often sinister and deadly nature of it all. There seems no evidence for the opposite, for the idea, our extraterrestrial "space brothers" did one single act of genuine generosity, kindness, or a single act of compassion.

The answer is, of course, there aren't any. However, there have been plenty of injuries, deaths, and disappearances, not to mention abductions and animal mutilations. That, in itself, should tell us something!

Therefore, it would behoove us to gather as much information about UFOs as we can. It would be to our advantage to build databases, as MUFON does, about the whole phenomenon. We should do our best to devise ways and means to protect our people from those extraterrestrials who might do us harm, but also from anyone else that might intend us such harm, as well.

We should advance our technologies as rapidly as possible, so any future interactions with such beings will be more evenhanded. In short, we have to take care of ourselves, take every reasonable precaution when it comes to all this, because it seems the extraterrestrials, and perhaps even our government will not do so.

So when and if you happen to see a UFO, don't just be amazed. Don't just be intensely curious. Rather, perhaps, you should be at least a little bit fearful, as well. In this case, such a thing might make for a good survival instinct for you and yours.

Remember when you look up and see a jet flying overhead, it doesn't mean we rule the skies, not at all. For something else seems to control that high ground.

Moreover, even if you aren't bothering to watch the skies, just remember, "they" still might be watching us. Sadly, that's exactly what they seem to be doing and all the time. Therefore, it is up to each of us to protect our families and ourselves, the best we can, and that requires knowledge, more of it. So if you see a UFO, report it! If it appears to be interacting with you, run! You may not get away, as so many do not, but at least, you can try.

If this seems unduly a gloomy conclusion, this can't be helped. Moreover, it's not meant to frighten or cause anyone to just give up and accept their fate. Rather, it's meant as a call to arms, a call to learn what we can, so we can better defend ourselves and our families against an unknown, but powerful enemy. The answer isn't to submit to them, but to challenge, and if necessary, fight them. If enough take this approach, maybe, just maybe, we won't be worth their time and effort anymore, and they might just leave us alone and go elsewhere. I think that would be a happy thing.

ABOUT THE AUTHOR

Rob Shelsky is an avid and eclectic writer, and averages about 4,000 words a day. Rob, with a degree in science, has written a large number of factual articles for the former AlienSkin Magazine, as well as for other magazines, such as Doorways, Midnight Street (U.K.), Internet Review of Science Fiction (IROSF), and many others. While at AlienSkin Magazine, a resident columnist there for about seven years, Rob did a number of investigative articles, including some concerning the paranormal, as well as columns about UFOs, including interviews of those who have had encounters with them.

Rob has been interviewed on a large number of shows, including George Noory's Coast-To-Coast AM Radio show, House of Mystery, The Kevin Cook Show, and many others. He has often and over a long period, explored the alien and UFO question and has made investigative trips to research such UFO hotspot areas as Pine Bush, New York, Gulf Breeze, Florida, and other such regions, including Brown Mountain, North Carolina, known, for the infamous "Brown Mountain Lights, as well as investigating numerous places known for paranormal activity. He has traveled abroad to do this, as well, as with traveling to sites in the United Kingdom, as well as other countries where UFOs have been reported. Rob is a member of MUFON, and a Field Investigator for this group.

With over 20 years of such research and investigative efforts behind him, Author Rob Shelsky is well qualified in the subject of UFOs, as well as that of the paranormal. Where Rob

Shelsky tends to be the skeptic, and insists upon being able to "kick the tires" of a UFO, to ascertain their reality, he is, as well, a theorist, constantly coming up with possible explanations for various such phenomena. Rob asks the hard questions others seem to avoid. Often, he comes up with convincing answers.

For links to Robs other books on the subject of UFOs, please go to:

http://home.earthlink.net/~robngeorge/

Or: http://robshelsky.blogspot.com/

Or: http://www.amazon.com/gp/search/ref=sr_tc_2_0?rh=i%3Astripbooks%2Ck%3ARob+Shelsky&keywords=Rob+Shelsky&ie=UTF8&qid=1298820526&sr=1-2-ent&field-contributor_id=B002BO9RIE

REFERENCES

1639 Abduction on Charles River, Boston:
http://www.celebrateboston.com/ufo/first-ufo-sighting.htm
Recent Survey on Number of Americans who believe the government is hiding information about UFOS:
http://www.usnews.com/news/articles/2012/06/28/most-americans-believe-government-keeps-ufo-secrets-survey-finds
http://en.wikipedia.org/wiki/UFO_conspiracy_theory
http://en.wikipedia.org/wiki/Virginia_Dare
http://ncpedia.org/culture/legends/virginia-dare
http://ufodigest.com/article/inexplicable-disappearance-village-qinling-mountains
http://www.ufosightingsdaily.com/2010/10/ufo-sighting-linked-to-entire-china.html
http://en.wikipedia.org/wiki/Angikuni_Lake
http://www.worldmysteriesandtrueghosttales.com/2009/08/strange-disappearance-of-anjikuni.html
http://www.cropcircleconnector.com/column/deadsea.html
http://www.disclose.tv/
http://www.theguardian.com/science/2014/nov/13/philae-comet-lander-alien-cover-up-conspiracy-theories-emerge
http://www.abovetopsecret.com/
http://www.mirror.co.uk/news/weird-news/roswell-ufo-conspiracy-explained-german-4436124
http://au.ibtimes.com/secret-space-programme-ufo-conspiracy-theorists-believe-nasa-constant-touch-aliens-1393199
http://www.dailymail.co.uk/sciencetech/article-2920426/Nasa-cuts-live-ISS-video-feed-UFO-hovers-sigh http://io9.com/5692584/6-real-life-alien-conspiracy-theories-even-more-unbelievable-than-fictionn-Conspiracy-theorists-claim-space-agency-hiding-alien-life.html
http://www.ufocoverup.org/

http://nymag.com/news/features/conspiracy-theories/harry-truman-aliens/
http://en.wikipedia.org/wiki/James_Forrestal
http://ufodigest.com/article/new-clue-james-forrestals-mental-problems-were-ufo-related
https://www.youtube.com/watch?v=_MrYl8ZYHmo
http://www.thelivingmoon.com/47john_lear/02files/The_UFO_Cover-up.html
http://www.v-j-enterprises.com/forestal.html
http://www.abovetopsecret.com/forum/thread432033/pg1
http://www.ufosightingsdaily.com/2012/01/ufo-caught-on-radar-causing-mass-bird.html
http://www.alienresistance.org/disclosure-project-death-destruction-caused-by-ufos/
http://en.wikipedia.org/wiki/Cattle_mutilation
http://www.ufo-disclosure.net/blog/are-ufo-researchers-being-targeted-with-cancer-causing-microwave-weapons
http://www.dailymail.co.uk/news/article-2220103/Man-photographs-UFO-dead-birds-appear-neighbours-garden.html
http://www.telegraph.co.uk/news/newstopics/howaboutthat/ufo/7555431/Unexplained-sheep-attacks-caused-by-aliens-in-UFOs-farmers-claim.html
http://www.colinandrews.net/UFO-UK-Sheep.html
http://www.ufodigest.com/mystery.html
http://www.huffingtonpost.com/2014/05/29/russian-yeti_n_5411705.html
http://en.wikipedia.org/wiki/Dyatlov_Pass_incident
http://www.dailymail.co.uk/news/article-2401175/Dyatlov-Pass-Indicent-slaughtered-hikers-Siberias-Death-Mountain-1959.html
http://www.cracked.com/article_16671_6-famous-unsolved-mysteries-with-really-obvious-solutions.html
http://mysteriousuniverse.org/2012/01/mountain-of-the-dead-the-dyatlov-pass-incident/
http://www.amazon.com/Dead-Mountain-Untold-Dyatlov-Incident/dp/1452112746
https://uk.news.yahoo.com/are-ufo-experts-being-murdered--new-book-to-investigate--pattern--of-deaths-134147932.html

http://www.google.com/url?sa=t&rct=j&q=&esrc=s&source=web&cd=4&ved=0CDUQFjAD&url=http%3A%2F%2Fwww.unknowncountry.com%2Fnews%2Funknowncountry-weekender-dangers-pursuing-truth-about-ufos&ei=7gDqVNWZL4WXgwTAzoOwBA&usg=AFQjCNFd5zLkSz_38zPpktwg5hi9EvOBNg&bvm=bv.86475890,d.eXY

http://english.pravda.ru/science/mysteries/12-10-2012/122435-ufo_researchers_die-0/

http://www.ufoevidence.org/documents/doc826.htm

http://doubtfulnews.com/2014/03/is-there-a-rash-of-ufo-researcher-deaths-just-because-im-paranoid/

http://www.abovetopsecret.com/forum/thread1002454/pg1

http://en.wikipedia.org/wiki/Unexplained_disappearances

http://en.wikipedia.org/wiki/List_of_people_who_disappeared_mysteriously

http://www.mnn.com/lifestyle/arts-culture/stories/15-famous-people-who-mysteriously-disappeared

http://www.mnn.com/lifestyle/arts-culture/stories/15-famous-people-who-mysteriously-disappeared

http://www.mnn.com/lifestyle/arts-culture/stories/15-famous-people-who-mysteriously-disappeared

http://www.unmuseum.org/triangle.htm

http://rt.com/news/russian-navy-ufo-records-say-aliens-love-oceans/

http://www.theoutpostforum.com/tof/showthread.php?1149-Top-Russian-Admirals-talk-about-UFOs

http://www.foxnews.com/story/2009/07/28/russian-navy-reveals-its-secret-ufo-encounters/

http://www.abovetopsecret.com/forum/thread484270/pg1

http://www.google.com/url?sa=t&rct=j&q=&esrc=s&source=web&cd=15&ved=0CDkQFjAEOAo&url=http%3A%2F%2Fwww.unknowncountry.com%2Fnews%2Frussian-documents-reveal-many-underwater-ufo-events&ei=mQLqVI_bOMmkgwSpmYPYCA&usg=AFQjCNHZSsI8slMTsMZ5pbYJENHF-jXBuQ

http://www.americanmonsters.com/site/2015/01/baikal-lake-humanoids-russia/

http://en.wikipedia.org/wiki/Crop_circle
https://www.youtube.com/watch?v=n1hM8mcoF-g
https://www.facebook.com/pages/Crop-Circles-UFOs-Ancient-Mysteries-Scientific-Speculations/246667595346687
http://www.ufos-aliens.co.uk/cosmiccrops.htm
http://www.ufos-aliens.co.uk/cosmiccrops.htm
http://en.wikipedia.org/wiki/Disappearance_of_Frederick_Valentich
http://www.google.com/url?sa=t&rct=j&q=&esrc=s&source=web&cd=12&ved=0CFoQFjAL&url=http%3A%2F%2Fwww.heraldsun.com.au%2Fnews%2Fvictoria%2Fufo-suspicions-still-cloud-disappearance-of-frederick-valentich%2Fstory-fni0fit3-1226875604542&ei=zwTqVK-lB4fEgwTuo4LwCw&usg=AFQjCNFBRBwY07U5fFXRBysbXhXxcXpX8A&bvm=bv.86475890,d.eXY
http://ufolinks4u2.blogspot.com/p/blog-page.html
http://www.google.com/url?sa=t&rct=j&q=&esrc=s&source=web&cd=12&ved=0CFoQFjAL&url=http%3A%2F%2Fwww.heraldsun.com.au%2Fnews%2Fvictoria%2Fufo-suspicions-still-cloud-disappearance-of-frederick-valentich%2Fstory-fni0fit3-1226875604542&ei=zwTqVK-lB4fEgwTuo4LwCw&usg=AFQjCNFBRBwY07U5fFXRBysbXhXxcXpX8A&bvm=bv.86475890,d.eXY
http://www.ufobc.com/kinross/persons/personsInvolved.html
http://outthere.podbean.com/e/kinross-incident-revisited/
https://unconventionalindividualist.wordpress.com/2008/01/23/top-100-ufo-cases/
http://www.collective-evolution.com/2013/03/02/ufos-deactivate-nuclear-missiles-around-the-world/
http://www.dailymail.co.uk/sciencetech/article-1315339/Aliens-hit-nukes-They-landed-Suffolk-base-claim-airmen.html
http://www.livescience.com/10146-ufos-disarm-nuclear-weapons.html
https://irenealia.wordpress.com/2012/10/13/many-ufo-researchers-die-under-mysterious-circumstances/
http://en.wikipedia.org/wiki/David_Paulides
https://www.youtube.com/watch?v=36v0ZAxahmk

http://ufos.about.com/od/aliensalienabduction/a/bestabductions.htm
http://www.ufocasebook.com/alienabductions.html
http://www.ufoevidence.org/topics/abduction.htm
https://www.youtube.com/watch?v=jcHxzZ4vMPs
http://www.ufosightingsdaily.com/2014/03/massive-ufo-pulls-up-to-space-station.html
http://en.wikipedia.org/wiki/2007_Alderney_UFO_sighting
http://www.dailymail.co.uk/news/article-463637/Mile-wide-UFO-spotted-British-airline-pilot.html
http://beforeitsnews.com/paranormal/2014/11/ufo-flying-over-paris-france-nov-2014-video-247
http://www.educatinghumanity.com/2013/12/ufo-sighting-france-video.html8594.html
http://en.wikipedia.org/wiki/Japan_Air_Lines_flight_1628_incident
http://www.ufosightingsdaily.com/2013/12/eight-ufos-seen-over-brooks-mountain.html
http://www.abovetopsecret.com/forum/thread444757/pg1
http://www.abovetopsecret.com/forum/thread444757/pg1
http://www.benningtontriangle.com/
http://www.reddit.com/r/UnresolvedMysteries/comments/2hh500/mysterious_disappearances_in_americas_national/
http://beforeitsnews.com/paranormal/2014/07/strange-disappearances-occurring-within-the-uni
http://www.messagetoeagle.com/missing411.phpted-states-national-parks-video-2472378.html
http://en.wikipedia.org/wiki/Vile_Vortices
http://www.strangerdimensions.com/2014/07/15/12-vile-vortices-ivan-sanderson/
https://www.google.com/search?q=Vile+vortices&ie=utf-8&oe=utf-8
http://www.veryhelpful.net/2014/12/devils_graveyards/
http
http://en.wikipedia.org/wiki/Ley_line://www.deepinfo.com/World Grid.htm
http://en.wikipedia.org/wiki/Ley_line
http://www.crystalinks.com/grids.html

http://www.ancient-wisdom.co.uk/leylines.htm